Poor Land
or Poor Minds:
Africa Respond!

By

Michel Ngue-Awane

MINA PUBLISHING

Table of Contents

Acknowledgements

To my wife, Annie.

You were with me when I had no job, and we rejoiced together when I landed my first job. We experienced frustration when I had difficulties obtaining my first contract after starting a business, and we both negotiated it together. 17 years have passed, and our blessings are now many. I told you that we would get there, if only we believed in ourselves.

We have achieved and surpassed all the goals we wanted to attain at this point in our lives. This book is a testimony to our determination to press on despite the setbacks. I firmly believe that everyone can be what they want to be. Now we can encourage many people who are on their journey, especially those who feel as frustrated as we were. We are still on a trip, but while we continue to strive for better, I can't stop saying; I love you, and thank you for your support.

Mum

To my Mum, Christine Djoumessi,

I say I love you. I rather say it now that you are still around. I celebrate you now, and I want you to be part of the celebration. I am blessed, having you around and I thank God for granting you good health. I thank you for being around and for raising me up.

To Nan, Lekeuneu,

I did not follow your tradition of naming after each of you. You all know that I challenge traditional thinking and status quo. However, I hope that you live longer through this book, particularly if it touches the lives of many.

Into the book

Human nature rejects poverty, and everyone can be successful; controversially, most people are deprived. This paradox caused by confusion and lack of understanding of the real source of wealth. Everyone who grasps the secret of success will always be better off. This secret is within everyone's reach. Your mind is the storehouse of success and failure and choices that you make are choices that make you. Although no one likes poverty, many people remain poor through personal choices.

People mistakenly think that a nation's natural resources determines how wealthy its citizens should be. Such assertions are not necessarily true because citizens create the wealth that makes the nation rich. Henceforth, resources are only discovered when people have awakened minds. Likewise, poverty is generated by a though and tit is a condition created by people. Poverty is not a natural condition.

To understand why people are rich or poor, we must understand how they think. An apparently poor land can become incredibly rich through man's actions. Equally, a land full of resources can be full of poor people. Examples of fertile lands with poor people are found everywhere in the world and particularly in Africa.

This confirms that poverty is created by a state of mind rather than the state of place. Any place, anywhere in the world can change its fortune with a change of people's mindset and the right application of knowledge.

People can make of a place what they want. Hence, the state of a place reflects its inhabitants' state of mind. A paradise can emerge in the middle of a jungle and a thriving and vibrant city can be transformed into a desolate land through man's actions.

The ability of an individual to think is a way by which he can enact and impose his will on earth. This means that any human being can change their social conditions by using his power within.

The power and the ability to think leads to self-discovery and a real learning will influence inspiration. The subconscious plays a crucial role in determining individual's social conditions. By registering positive thoughts and reflecting them outwardly as a concrete manifestation of needs and wants, derives better living standards with their outward manifestations. Pure inspiration and pure forms come from the eternal and immutable forms that rest in a human's spirit.

The present book is for everyone who wants to achieve his potential. A book for everyone who intends to get out of his shell and break the barriers of self-limitation. In this book, you will discover the causes of poverty and how to overcome them.

Everything created is conceived in mind. Consequently, the solution to overcome poverty must focus on a mind transformation programme. For Africa to regain its place of predilection as a thinker, Africans must change the way they think. A change of their mindset will pave their way out of poverty.

Poverty in the continent is a sign of Africans' self-betrayal, as they try to live other people's lives, following the crowd, resigning to fate and believing little in themselves.

Beyond Africa, this book shows that each human being can be a success and achieve beyond measure by using their mind and using it well.

You are a success even if you ignore your worth!

Chapter 1

Human Nature Rejects Poverty

Carelessly walking but carefully choosing their places among the sea of sunbathers, each visitor to the beach laid down their towels on the glistening sand, as overloaded itinerant merchants walked past, chanting "for sale", as they showcased the goods they held in their hands.

These wayfaring Merchants were like walking shops and carried all their supplies and treasures with them. One could say that they were both mobile warehouses and stores. This way of life was unique to Africa!

These purveyors chose the beach because it is a perfect spot for potential high paying customers. To foreign tourists, they could sell their goods 100 times more than the regular price. One such deal could cover two months' profit.

Bars and mini fish restaurants lined the beach. Not everyone could secure a spot for business in this part of the town.

Fotetsa beach was a prime food business district, even though each restaurant has a limited menu choice. They offered only fish or chicken, with plantain or mashed cassava paste called "Bobolo" or "miniondo" as both main course and desert. Occasionally, a pint of beer substituted the starter and the dessert.

On approaching the beach, you could feel fresh air, caused by energy passing through the water that made the water to move in a circular motion. The waves released a fresh summer's breeze, wafting the delicious scent of grilled fish and roast chicken towards beachgoers and tourists, visibly tempting them to buy the delicious treats.

Seagulls circled the beach like vultures. Occasionally, they punched on an empty crisp packet or fallen grilled fish, only to be scared away by either intrigued children running around with angry or cheerful parents chasing after them, or courtesans and lovers walking and brazenly kissing, as older people seating by the bars cringed in disgust and complained about how the times had changed.

Scuttling along the sea-stained sand, unfortunate crabs venturing around stood no chance of escaping, as each visitor was a potential angler, ready to catch any edible creature that flaunted around.

Wielding her flimsy pink net, a young girl of around five perched on a boulder was laughing joyously as other children of similar age scattered other peoples' sandcastles when running around like headless chickens, with older brothers or sisters chasing behind to catch them before they drowned in the deep sea.

Elsewhere in the same beach, a young boy laughed as the waves lapped at his feet as he starred happily at his collection of shells.

On a cliff high above the beach stood Ben and his son Kem, who had left their mansion to visit this area, well known for gathering the deprived.

Kem had always wondered why so many of his fellow citizens were so poor while his dad had everything he wanted, and much more than he needed.

This visit only created more interrogations in Kem's mind despite his anticipated hope of getting answers. Perhaps, it was his dad's wish to provoke such thoughts in Kem's mind. If this was the case, surely, he had some answers for Kem on the principles of wealth creation and the causes of poverty around them-in Africa.

From the cliff, Kem and his dad were chatting while looking at the beach.

Closer to the shore, they observed two teenagers carelessly floating on a pair of old bright pink lilos before suddenly breaking out in laughter, then falling off.

They gave many trials, giving up not as amateur surfers sand scene continued for a while A great wind blew from the shore, carrying the scent of grilled fish toward the teenagers-and certainly triggered a reaction as they became visibly hungry, hence, they dragged their lilos to the coast, intending on coercing their parents into opening their wallets. Even from afar, their intentions were discernible.

Noticing this, and almost convinced of their intentions, Kem, yelled "hello", waving towards the teenagers. The teens looked up and rubbed their tummies, thus making their intension clearer. After all, begging from strangers was common in this part of the world. Everyone expected someone to give them something for free and there was no shame asking for help or support even from strangers.

Kem continued: "Hello, do you want anything? I can see that you are hungry". On hearing this word, the teenagers' faces brightened, and they became excited and eager to listen to what Ben had to say to them. "Here is some money for you"!

He lobbed down some coins and notes in local currencies to the teenagers, who rushed to pick them up. Noticing Kem's gesture, other children and even adults standing nearby rushed to pick theirs. Soon the whole beach was alerted of the "manna" falling from the cliff. It did not take them long to notice that the gift was coming from Ben, the richest man in the land and his son Kem, who were standing up.

People were cheering, and mostly happy for the privilege of seeing Ben in person. Ben was well known, not only for his wealth but also for his generosity. Many people present on that day had only heard about Ben but had never seen him in person and considered themselves privileged to see him face to face.

Everyone now rushed beneath the cliff, with many trying to climb to reach Ben's height begging for more coins.

Unfortunately, rain began to fall on the beach, awakening sunbathers and scattering all beachgoers, including those who were waiting beneath the cliff for Ben's coins. As people started to pack up and leave, the rain grew heavier, causing bikini-clad girls to scream and take cover under umbrellas and food stalls.

Kem beseeched his dad to let him visit the bar where most people had taken refuge to escape the rain. Dad, who grew up in a similar environment, had no problem agreeing to his son's request.

As they entered the bar, everyone stood up, amazed by their presence. It was not in Ben's habits to visit pubs, local bars or restaurants. His visit was therefore a delightful surprise for both visitors and the restaurant's owner.

When they entered the bar, Ben offered a drink and food to everyone. It was a great day of business for the restaurant owners. Not only did they double their prices, but they also sold out.

Every person who was at the beach that afternoon ate and drank as long as there was supply.

Ben was incredibly generous, and money spent on that day could not, in any way affect his wealth. As people feasted, they could not thank Ben enough. You could hear words like "may God continue to bless you, sir", "your supply will never run dry, sir", "may you never lack". "You are different from other rich people", "you are not like white people who have ruined our country". "Western people have over-exploited our continent and thank God we have a local citizen like you who have redeemed us". "The westerners always take, without giving anything back to the community. Not even a simple drink like you are doing now, God will punish them"!

As soon as one person had the courage to utter insults on Europeans, accusing them of being responsible for their poverty, others followed with moaning about how their land had been over-exploited by them. It was the beginning of unending commotions and complaints about how the west duped Africans. As they continued to do so, the whole mood and debate changed. Now, everyone joined in with a series of unending hullabaloos, bitterness and cursing of the Westerners, whom they blamed for their misery and poverty. Faced with these complaints, Ben was compelled to give a word of counsel. He knew more than anyone else did that anyone could overcome poverty and that complaining will never change anything.

From his personal experience, Ben contended that the causes of poverty were inherent to an individual. He maintained that every single individual could become whatever they want to become if they want. As he took centre stage with Kem by his side, he gave the following advice:

"My fellow friends, from today, I want you to stop moaning about your situation. Instead, change your mindset. You alone can do something about your life. Everyone lives for self; however, the consequence of their actions affects others either positively or negatively. If you are determined, you can change the course of your lives. You can overcome barriers and traps set up by the anyone to limit and exploit you.

"I want you to stop complaining that foreigners are the cause of your demise. Even though they may have some degree of responsibilities, you remain the master of your destiny.

Choices that you make are choices that make you. Your mind is yours alone, and you determine what goes in. What you let sink into your mind determines how you think, act, and behave. If you want to overcome limitations orchestrated by others to dominate you, you must first change your mindset. You need to find the real causes of poverty within yourself. You must stop accusing other people of doing what you can control and stop blaming people for your condition. Blame and accusations will not move you an inch forward. Only your action will determine your next destination. Let your discovery of injustices become the reason behind your determination to change and success.

"You need to look at yourself and ask yourself a question: Why, despite sharing and inheriting the same past, some of your fellow citizens are better off than yourselves? You need to do a self-assessment and seek answers from within. You are complaining that your resources have been- and are still being- stolen by the west. However, instead of complaining, I exhort you to think creatively in order find the best way to add value to your country's natural resources".

"You may start by your land's resources and think creatively about how you could exploit them to meet people's needs. Tell me, what exploratory machines or techniques have you invented to discover or to transform your resources? Do you have a plan or vision to manage those resources? If you treasure your resources, you should make it your first and most important priority to transform them by yourselves and in your land. I am not saying that you should give your natural resources away for free. I am just asking you to find a way in which you could make a better use of them. If you do not, you will probably continue to complain in the next few hundred years.

Resources in their raw or natural state are of little use. Resources cannot self-transform. If you cannot add value to your natural resources, you probably have no choice, but to settle with the offer you are given by those who have discovered them, and who know what to do with them, those who know how to transform them. Your land can be full of resources, but they will bring you no benefits if you didn't know they existed, or their importance".

"If you only look at finished products, you have missed the key. Before you see anything in its physical form, a lot of work had already taken place in someone's mind to make it happen. A product is conceived before it is made. Many people believe that man is a physical being only, and therefore they only look for material things, hoping that material things will change their lives.

In a desire to satisfy the needs of the body, there is the tendency to lose sight of man' potential to know things, conceive, invent and create. Only humans' creative power changes their life from within. We should not live in ignorance or wilful neglect of our true self. You are a spirit, soul and body and the real self, eternal and immortal, is Spirit".

The 'Body' belongs to the material world experienced through the five senses of 'Sight,' 'Smell,' 'Hearing,' 'Taste' and 'Touch.' The 'Soul' is 'Imagination,' 'Conscience,' 'Memory,' 'Reason' and the 'Affections, and the "Spirit" receives impressions of outward material things through the soul. The spiritual faculties of the 'Spirit' are 'Faith,' 'Hope,' 'Reverence' and 'Prayer' which is the sphere of God-consciousness.

"The realm where the work of regeneration takes place, and where a man can connect with the stable and unchangeable source of life and truth-God is spiritual. A man is Spirit in the image of God, with God's faculties. Therefore, he can do all things that he wills to do and be what he wants depending on his will power or his willingness without wavering. This is otherwise called faith. The spirit is the element of humanity that gives us the ability to have an intimate relationship with the immutable-God. Whenever the word "spirit" is used, it refers to the immaterial part of humanity that "connects" with God, who Himself is Spirit (John 4:24).

"So, if you want to improve your life, you need to make good use of your Spirit. I will use mind here, to refer to the dimension of Soul and Spirit because this interaction determines what you manifest outwardly.

"Those who are dominated by the soul are prone to errors, passions, wrong and evil. But those who act according to the spirit are likely to succeed and pursue good.

Remember that the soul is in the middle of the body and the spirit, which is pure good and truth and should guide therefore all our desires coming from the body through the soul. If your mind is in control, you will never go wrong. But naturally, the soul and body's urges are louder than the spirit'. Led by the soul and the body, man is prone to errors, wrong choices, envy, jealousy, arrogance, greed, and all sorts of evil. The mind is therefore where your life can be improved or destroyed.

"You were created with a mind, and through the power of your imagination, you can make discoveries to fulfil your needs. Your mind is your only tool you can use to create your wealth.

With a rich mind, you can create a productive life. Your mind is your sure way to a better life and freedom. Your mind is a source of wealth and success. Only through your mind, can you make your life better and leave your mark on this world. You can only transform the world through a better application of your mind.

If you lose your mind, you have wasted your life, and you will be of no use to yourself or others. With a weak mind, you are a poor man or woman. No one will mind you if you are mindless. Henceforth, to be given certain responsibilities or to be appointed in top jobs, you must be considered of sound mind.

"Your mind will determine your wealth, your position and your contribution to fellow humans. Only through your mind can you make a difference. Your mind is the tool that will help you shape your world, and consequently the world in general.

"For over a hundred years, Africans have been crying out loud for being duped by the West. Their cries were the reason they fought for independence, and seventy years after the independence, Africans are still complaining.

Are Africans still being duped? I certainly think so, but why? The onus is on them to find an answer to this question, and not on those who are duping them.

"I contend that, if Africans are fooled, it is because they are making the wrong judgements concerning their affairs. If they are duped, it is because they are running away from their responsibilities. Their blaming game is a cheap substitute for action. It is just a consolation.

"Bad application of the mind brings bad results. Bad judgement produces bad outcomes. Instead of moaning, it is wise to understand the causes of your current situation and find the best way to improve it. Unless this self-assessment is carried out, Africans will continue to be duped and undoubtedly continue to cry.

"Our mind is the only tool that is at our disposal to counter-attack hidden agendas and soft methods of dupery. If we can easily be duped, it just means that we do not apply our judgement right; consequently, our competitors or detractors jump on the opportunity to make the best out of our ignorance.

"We can do the same. We can find a way to get the results that we want, by affirming ourselves as master of our destiny. We can get a solution to our problems. Such stance and endeavour require sacrifices and a dedication of time and resources. Life is pure and obedient. It gives to you what you ask of it. Your attitude toward the world will determine the kind of life you live.

Your life and your place in the world are in your hands. Contrary to what you hear from the multitude, life does not dictate your attitude. You can dictate how your will experience life. By changing your mindset, you will change your attitude, and the change of attitude is the easiest, most certain, and permanent route to changing your life. Do not go through life tied to your family's history or your past. It is hard to move on holding to the past. You are not a crab; you are a human who looks forward and not backwards. Your mistakes, mishaps, imperfections, and ego are like shadows that you should look and laugh at. Consider them as necessary in shaping your present character and instead of moaning, use them as a learning curve.

"Even as we speak, you have not finished learning, at least when you are still physically present in the world. The quest for better and new should be your daily drive. You should invest regularly in your human capital, by developing your ability and talents, through continuous education. Education will stretch your mind and help you to find solutions to problems. The beach is right, but most of you spend all your days on this beach. What a waste!

There is a lot to do in the world, and here you can find a solution to one of the world most pressing issues, but how can you do that when you only care about your daily survival? You can discover things that matter to the world. Although your land is productive, none of you has identified any of its natural resources. Your inability to proactively explore your land to (or "intend to") identify existing resources highlights your level of complaisance with life. Your idleness highlights your inability to stretch your mind.

"One more discovery can save the whole of humanity, but this will not be possible if you spend your time sunbathing and complaining about others. Those who have made significant discovery have done so through sacrifice and dedication. They would not have done it if they had stopped at their last exploit. You can do the same and as you thrive for more and for better, keep control of your thoughts. Your thoughts are a seed for your tomorrow. The rest of your life depends on the quality of your thoughts. Your thoughts are pregnant with the rest of your life. My favourite song is the S Club 7, *Reach for the stars*.

"You can reach the stars. There is no limit above your head. The cloud you see is just another space, and you can climb higher than what you see. You can rise to any height you're willing to jump. You have potential and ability. So, don't stop, don't settle yet".

"You will have greater visibility from the highest heights. From the bottom, you cannot see anything because it is overcrowded. From the bottom, your visibility is obstructed by hindrance and a confused crowd. There are too many people at the bottom, and with your small stature, it is even more difficult for you to see around the corner. I say so because you are not from a nation of giants. You are of a small stature like me. So, jump or climb like Zacchaeus. From a treetop or a "sycamore tree", you will not only be able to see the source of life, but all will see you.

"When Zacchaeus climbed the tree, he saw Jesus, so, was he seen by everyone passing by. This courageous act put him in the spotlight, hence, he is still known today. Many lived during Zacchaeus's time, but they are not remembered. Zacchaeus is remembered for his climbing on the tree as an example to follow by everyone who wants to succeed in something. Zacchaeus rose above the crowd. Perhaps by climbing like Zacchaeus, you will become the star everyone will aim to reach. Start the ascension right now. Use your mind to find the right strategy for your ascension".

"Your mind is indiscriminate. It absorbs whatever you feed it. It retains the filth as well as the noble, but the filth will corrupt the noble, and corrupt your whole mind with the dirt it absorbs. So, fill it with ideas, thoughts and images you would want to have reflected in the mirror of your life. So, make up your mind, to make of your life, what you want it to be. It is your duty without fail. If you miss this call, you have missed your goal and failure will follow. I am sure you do not want to be poor, and even if you think you are poor, I hope you do not want to remain so! If you lack inspiration, you can draw it from the source. The source is reachable in the realm of the spirit, where the truth is immutable, and the realities are pure and permanent".

"There is a dimension much greater than what you can see with your eyes, and there is pure love that seeks nothing in return that resides in the realm of the spirit. This source of life and love should be your inspiration. This source is real. It is good, and it is God-your mind. He is in and for you if you want your mind to be his dwelling place.

He can only manifest if you put him first. If he is first, everything else will fit into the right place, at the right time and in the right amount. In fact, you will have no struggle, and your mind will be pure and fruitful".

"Look around and see what I have achieved. I did not fall from the sky. I was born in the same land as you but in a much worse time. If I could do it, so can you. Believe it, see it, and it is yours. You can get everything you want, provided you have no doubt. This means seeing it in your spirit. Once you have done this, it is yours, and you will see its physical manifestation".

"For me, no human being of a sound mind should be poor. Moreover, Africa, the land of the first intelligent man should not be full of poor people. Nobody should be hungry in a continent full of resources like Africa."

"Opportunities are many in Africa and Africans shouldn't be dying of hunger. Almost all Africans are landowners, but paradoxically they are poorer than a church mouse. Despite their reputation of having active support networks and their legendary hospitality, they are rooted in greed, self-centredness, and selfishness. Why is this so? Africa's poverty comes down to a mindset of its people; their shared and collective mindset creates a state of permanent lack.

Although their pretend to dislike poverty, most of them remain poor, not through anyone else's fault but through personal choices. The unconscious programming of their mind produces a visible impact on their living conditions. Fortunately, like every human being, each African has the potential for great success. Each African is potentially and in principle a miracle. Their potential is unlimited; the only problem is their lack of action with severe consequences.

"The individual achievement has ramifications in the world's chain of exchanges. As such, anyone who fails to contribute to this chain is a cheat, a fraudster who lives on borrowed terms"

"In fact, those type of people are living "borrowed lives", and you do not want to be one of them. Tune in for self-discovery if you want to make an impact. Nothing is impossible. The yet unthinkable and unimaginable is possible once the glimpse of it had filtered through your mind. This is the theory of human possibilism: nothing is impossible, or all things are possible. My theory of human illimitationism asserts that there are no limits to what people can perceive and achieve".

"The actual extent of the mind's abilities is yet to be discovered and tested. We will probably not understand this for some time. A man is still unable to use even a tenth of his abilities. When we reach a state where our mind is used to its maximum, this theory will be tested and re-evaluated. For now, it remains irrefutable."

Ben's advice is for every human being who wants to achieve his potential; for every person who intends to get out of his shell and break the barriers of self-limitation. It is not just about Africans' betrayal of themselves. It is not just about Africans living other peoples' lives, as they follow the crowd, resigning to fate and believing little in themselves; rather it is about what human beings can achieve.

If you had almost given up, I urge you to stand up, pick you your loads and move! You can do it. You can be what you want to become and achieve success beyond any man's expectations. You are a creator and master of your destiny. You determine what you get from life, and your thoughts and actions have a great impact on your future. You chose what you leave as a legacy, and your history is what you make of your life. It is therefore up to you to create and define how you want it to be, and what you want to be remembered for.

Paradise or hell is a choice that you hold, hence if your aim is to live in heaven, you need to choose. It is a fallacy to think that poverty on earth will lead you to heavenly paradise.

If you cannot experience paradise here on earth, I doubt you will live it in heaven. You create your heavens through you action here on earth and beyond.

If you miss creating those conditions while on earth, you will surely not experience paradise in heaven. What you taste here will multiply there! If you are unable to have a glimpse of hope and success here on earth, you are probably on the wrong track and have missed the mark. Those who miss the mark also miss their way.

Whether you are a believer or not, if you are suffering here on earth, it means that you are disconnected to the source- the truth, the right way, which you can know, if you are inspired by the infinite in you can do the impossible and overcome lack-poverty. You have and should have the spirit of the omnipotent, omniscient, and eternal guiding you from within. In 1 John 2:27 (NIV) we can read; "As for you, the anointing you received from him remains in you, and you do not need anyone to teach you. But as his anointing teaches you about all things and as that anointing is real, not counterfeit—just as it has taught you, remain in him."

Having the spirit of the omnipotent implies that you are potentially omnipotent. This is the true meaning of being made in the image of God. You are Godlike according to Geneses 1:27, in Romans 8:14 and John 16:13; "For all who are led by the Spirit of God are sons of God."

"When the Spirit of truth comes, he will guide you into all the truth, for he will not speak on his authority, but whatever he hears he will speak, and he will declare to you the things that are to come". You can have access to the source of knowledge and can know what to do always and in every circumstance is you wish, and if you are doing the right things, you will get the good results.

Poverty and suffering come from doing the wrong things and how can you reach paradise by doing the bad things? How can you pass your exam by giving the wrong answers? How can you succeed either on earth or in heaven if you have spent your time on earth doing the wrong things? Therefore, I say that your paradise starts on earth.

This is not fiction. It is the truth. Just as some people have achieved wonders, you too can! Once you are connected, you will discover the right path to everything that can improve your life here on earth. Once you are connected, you will find the secret to success and happiness, and scarcity will become history.

If you do not know your way here, you are lost, much less living the way you were supposed to live. Once again, everything is up to you. You have a choice as to how you live your life: 1 John 4:4 says that "But you belong to God, my dear children. You have already won a victory over those people because the Spirit who lives in you is greater than the spirit who lives in the world." So, you can draw a source of inspiration and guidance from within- by your mind, which is connected to the infinite Spirit, if you are in tune with Him.

Once again, you decide, but the path you take will determine what you will become. Your purpose is designed, but your destiny is in your hands. You are equipped at birth with potential. It is up to you to discover and use your gifts. The path you create leads to a destination: this is what we call destiny. The choice is yours!

Everything you need is waiting for you to discover it, so you can make use of it and help others. Discoveries can be made anywhere in the world. There are probably more needs in Africa. Consequently, there is a greater urgency for developments in Africa. With all its potential and natural resources, there is no reason why Africa should be deprived. It is not anyone else's fault. It is Africans' own choice, be it unconscious or not. I am certain beyond any doubt that their demise is unconsciously created by themselves.

As you discover your latent power within, as you find your illimitationism, your limitless possibilities, as you see your true essence as a perfect being, and as you discover your potential, the might and the extent to what you can become, tap into it and spring forth. You are a miracle that is unaware of your true self.

You can create and to access an unlimited source of supplies. Creativity and discoveries belong to all human beings. You have the right to this. You don't have to feel guilty when using findings from China or Europe if you are playing your part and contributing.

If you contribute to the circle of giving and receiving, you are surely playing your part. We rely on each other. Each person must fulfil their duties, but to do what you are called to do, you need to discover who you are as well as your unique gifts and talents. You must be conscious of your abilities, your potential, and you must have a vision, passion, and dedication to reaching your goals. In simple terms, to be who you want to be, you must know who you are and what you want to become before finding out what you need to do to get there.

Chapter 2

The Discovering Self and Our Individuality

It was around the 5th hour of the day. The sky was painted a bright blue, and the bright green grass glistened in the sun announcing a great day for Mengang market traders.

The white clouds from the cold night had gradually faded as the sun climbed towards its zenith. The wind was dwindling, and the songs of the birds seldom heard at this time of the day. Everyone anticipated fervently for the village market to open on Saturdays. This was the best market in the whole county. The market square was well known in the entire region, and some sellers were famous for their produce.

Mengang market attracted people from as far as Santchou, Ngwata, Bale-Mankan, Fondonera, Foguetafo, Bamia, Melong, Barre, Mouangel, and Sekou. Even people from Mboroukou and Melong came to sell their provisions at the market. Some people simply came to enjoy the atmosphere.

From dawn, people started making their way to the village square, which hosted this weekly market. By 8 am, the market was crammed with people, goods and livestock were ready to be sold as the village's peaceful slumber of the night before had completely vanished. It is amazing how quickly a place can change. In this panacea of human, animals, and cargos, it was hot and constricted as people continued to pour in. The peak and busiest time was between 11 am – 3 pm. Between these hours the market roared with rage.

At peak time, the market was so busy that people had to walk in a straight file like soldiers going to battle, or pensioners queuing in Africa's social security services for their penny copper pension. Here and there, market stalls lined the market square obediently. None of them had doors, and when they had one, they wouldn't last long against the might, impatience, and violence of customers, who travelled from afar each week to buy goods that could only be found in Mengang market. So, to be served first, some customers removed everything hindering their passage.

Whether in Rimtounda Tchapalo's brewery or Massa Martin Soya Palace, herds of people climbed on top of each other, yelling wildly like mindless monkeys brawling for a banana as each of them wanted to be served first, regardless in which order they came or in. It did not matter who came first. Even the last person to arrive wanted to be served before those they met there. There was no concept of queues and no consideration for others. What mattered was "I". Each wanted their needs to be met. That was it! You could hear people screaming: "I was the first", "you jumped the queue", "please give me my change" etc. Even though there were always enough provisions for everyone, no one had the patience to wait their turn. They were born and bred in a culture where patience was not a virtue.

Large, tattered crafter waggons, made of wood, decorated with a collage of vegetables, were parked beside the street. Their owners stood beside them screaming prices like auctioneers, but instead of a hammer, they had carrots, potatoes, avocados, yams, onions, corn, and cabbage. They used their goods to shoo away the flies dancing around the vegetables or to invite passers-by to visit their stalls.

Sweaty buyers skilfully wove their way through the minute gaps between people to their next stall, while pickpockets felt like rabbits in a carrot field, and munched purses out of many pockets of innocent buyers too busy bargaining. But when they were caught, they were burnt alive or lynched to death in the market square. In this atmosphere, experienced visitors wore tight pants for the same reason - to hide their cash from these petty thieves.

It was easy to see helpless drunkards fumble through the scores of bags or hit the edges of the waggons parked by the roadside. Some of these drunks swayed side to side, forcing their way through the crowd. When they were still lucid, they were making their way to the next kwata shop for more odontol or alcoholic Bisap so skilfully brewed by Rimtounda and his fellow villagers.

As the sun continued to warm the market, the stuffy air smelled of sweat and rotting food released a foul scent. The smells were so strong that no air freshener could have defeated their rancid stink. But none of these odours were enough to keep visitors away from the market.

The heat of the sunny afternoon flamed the market with exhaustion, as breathlessness silently took its toll on the visitors. Regular visitors to the market had become used to the atmosphere and continued to shop whiles fighting against the torture of heat and exhaustion.

The deafening chaos in the market made ears split. It seemed as if you were in a crowded nightclub. As most vendors continued to yell prices, frustrated customers angrily argued with annoyed sellers. It seemed as if all the sounds in the world had come to a reunion. From as far as three miles away from the square, Ben Sekou could hear this tumultuous brouhaha. In this melting pot, people kept shopping, chatting, arguing, or fighting until late.

Indeed, the square was furious on market days even throughout the night, unlike other days where at nightfall, it became lifeless and as silent as a graveyard with the moonlight faintly escaping through the huddle of clouds draping the moon as the market slept deeply. Again, and again, the square was always ready to explode at the first sign of light every Saturday. Seldom had people noticed this market's real beauty and enchantment or understood its secrets.

How and when was this market created? None of its living visitors knew; its date of inception had never been written anywhere. Had Mengang's market changed? The most pressing question for those who dared was: Had the people of Mengang made the best of it? It is hard to tell. One thing was sure, Mengang market was older than the people who sold goods and shopped there. With long forgotten secrets lying deeply buried in its roots, it kept on living, and people kept on selling and shopping there even though nothing stopped it from moving on.

Every Saturday, it was the same and usual humdrum, Mengang market square was the centre of focus where everyone who was old enough to join the buying and selling, the sharing of kwata, odontol, palm wine, chapalo or the best alcoholic Bisap converged. The alcoholic, Bisap was a masterpiece of Rimtounda, the master brewer of Mengang.

Rimtounda was a halogen whose parents came from Zagtouli located on the outskirts of Ouagadougou. They migrated over 30 years ago when Rimtounda was still a boy, following a prolonged drought in their village to settle in Mengang and never returned. After all, they were citizens of the world and could make their home wherever they felt comfortable. Rimtounda senior, the father died and was buried in Mengang and news was sent to the family back home in Zagtouli to inform them that he was no more. It is not sure the news ever reached them. After his death, his children born in Mengang had no reason to go back to their ancestral land. Perhaps they will do this one day.

This Saturday was special in Mengang. It was the king's daughter's poug-poug-som, the bridal ceremony. So, it was more than a day for usual shopping and enjoyment. A lot of free drinks were on the horizon due to the upcoming bridal ceremony, and people loved free drinks. Hence the day was highly anticipated.

On this day, Ben had been left at home with his brothers and sisters. In this part of the world, there was no fear of leaving children home alone and children as young as two years old were regularly left alone at home with siblings, food left at the child's reach.

Ben's brothers and sisters were lucky because he was already nine years old. At nine, he was probably the oldest child left alone at home to look after his siblings. Other kids, younger than him, were at the market selling goods with their parents or helping on subsistence farms. However, despite selling or working all year long, they experienced unending starvation. They had inherited poverty and hunger and were prolonging this legacy.

From their home, Ben could hear noises from the market and people merchandising: "three for fifty-cent apples, water for sale, oil, soy for sale". It was like chaos in the market. Everyone was talking; negotiating prices of goods, fighting and some people were naturally merry. Many people seized the opportunity to arrange their son's or daughter's marriage. Whatever they were saying, it was difficult for Ben to hear and make sense of the conversations.

Up to that day, Ben was living, just living! One could say that he was just a living soul. Ben was completely unaware of things that indeed went on around him or inside of him. Not that he could not talk or walk. Not that he was unable to see or hear. Not that he did not have the ability to act, accept or refuse to do things, or that he couldn't think. He felt to some extent. He had his mind.

He was able, up to then, to say no or yes; he could do things that he was asked to do or refuse to do it as he saw fit. In fact, it appeared as if he didn't lack understanding. He knew his family, neighbours, and friends. We could say that he was able to process information to the best of his abilities notwithstanding his youthful age. He was developing as was anticipated of a person of his age; in fact, he was possibly more mature than most children of his age group, and people often said that he was very astute. Despite his development, he was somehow "unconsciously unconscious" of the real meaning of life. His ability to make sense of his existence was limited; furthermore, he was unable to apprehend his better and deeper self. We could say that he was guided from without, rather than from within, and had not yet started to use his mind to direct the course of his life.

He was living by what he saw, touched, tasted, heard, smelt, and felt. He was living by his senses. He had not yet understood that reality was beyond sensual perception and had not yet made a difference between himself and the outer world. It could be said that he was unable to think properly or that he could not be trusted to make sound decisions. Ben was not yet in touch with his infinite source of pure thoughts creativity and sublime power within himself. Perhaps, only his body and soul guided his life as his not yet had a conscience of his spiritual dimension.

Though his inner power was limitless, Ben was still unaware of it. He had this potential, but he had not realised it yet. He could make his life what he wished but he wasn't aware yet, despite having the power of will. Ben had not yet reached this realisation. This is how many people live their lives, from birth to death.

Despite existing in total ignorance of his latent abilities, Ben was a happy little boy. This inability to grasp the extent of their potential and hidden power was typical in this part of the world. Most adults living in this village were unable to grasp the might of their spiritual wealth and the extent of their role in shaping their lives. They ignored the principles that could enable them to change their living conditions. Some people living similarly spend their entire lives looking outwardly for answers to issues pertaining to their lives and destinies. No wonder they could not find them or make any impact in the world.

The only difference between Ben and some of the older people living in the village was that they were stronger physically. Notwithstanding their physical strength, they were still in their infancy, living in total ignorance of the fundamental principles of life and it purpose. Why were they here on earth? They were unable to ask or answer this question since their existence was focussed on their daily survival. Consequently, instead of living, their life was frenzied by the need to survive.

Before this day, Ben had not pondered over his life, his destiny, his origins, or his future. He was just existent and was mimicking others without clearly understanding what he was doing. Ben was living! At home he was happy; he was playing as usual with his siblings.

On this day, he had a sudden and hasty awakening in his mind. He realised he was! He became conscious of self, his individuality and existence.

Just as he was coming to terms with this discovery, a gentle wind blew as joyful sounds of the marketplace caught his attention once again. There was a lot of noise from the market square. The market sellers were happier and became forgetful of their good manners having sold their goods and drank countless glasses of chapalo, kwata, odontol or alcoholic Bisap. Cries of joy and sorrow were heard here and there, and Ben could discern such commotions from his home.

As he had suddenly become conscious, his first question was, why were these villagers not thinking about their future? Why were they not bothered about the exact reasons for their presence here on earth? Why was the enjoyment of the present moment most important for these villagers than anything else?

To help villagers live in their permanent hibernation, Rimtounda kept them captive with his opiate Bisap. They were simply happy; happy! They had inherited this sense of happiness from their fathers, who got it from their fathers, and ancestors, and so on. Drink, food and sex were all they cared about. As this blind living continued, the village remained almost the same years on.

People who knew the community said that the village had not changed; nothing new or particularly good had ever happened in the village as long as they could remember. The market had not changed much, people's behaviour had not changed either, hunger had not stopped, and people's conditions had not improved. Roads had not expanded, and houses had not changed forms. Improvements to the villagers' conditions had been very slow, yet billions had changed hands in Mengang market. However, elsewhere on the planet, tremendous progress was taking place.

For hours, Ben could hear people crying and fighting as result of taking too much of Rimtounda's drink as people sang and cried after drinking to excess. At first, Ben could not understand why an atmosphere of apparent joy and excitement could suddenly turn sour, hence his multiple questions on the real meaning of life. This was the real world in which he lived. He needed to get used to this reality. The market atmosphere was not new! It had always been like that; however, on this day, on this occasion, something new had taken place in Ben's mind. He had suddenly awakened.

He had started to make sense cf the world and the environment outside of himself. He had begun to perceive and discern his individuality. This was an internal process; it was frightening and astonishing. The awareness of his inner self made him feel lonely and even frightened. It was an inexplicable, yet significant moment for him.

Without warning, he knew that his life was his, in his hand. His mind was separate from others, what he thought was within him and he understood this because he, analogically could not perceive what was in his siblings' minds, at that time. It looked as if each was a closed vase, a closed container in which content was only discernible, perceivable by the container itself and what was seen from the outside or by the outside world was only what the container wanted the outsiders to see. So what people see could be fake, not real, twisted or a wilful display of what the person wanted others to see. One could be laughing while crying from within. One could be crying while joyful from within. Outsiders will see someone's laughter or screams as reality, whereas, in fact, it is not. In this regard, it could be said the real person is what he thinks. The real is in mind, and the real person is his spirit.

Ben had perceived the real him, though he could touch his body, he realised that he only made sense of his body, called it so from his mind. So, without his mind, he was probably not! This was the beginning of a turning point in his life. A brand-new chapter was opening for him. He had been alive for 9 years; the same scenario was always on the menu every Saturday in the market square with all appearing normal up to this point. This Saturday, for the first time, there was a click inside of him, that, up to then, he had been unaware of. A conscience! This is what distinguishes humans from animals. The conscience is this ability to be aware of and responding to one's surroundings, the capacity of the mind or a thought directly perceptible to and under the control of the person concerned.

This self-discovery was sudden, appeared without warning as Ben just instantly knew he was! Now, without a doubt, he knew and understood that he was. This discovery highlighted his individuality as compared to the others; the self and others like him without being him. The separateness between him and the world in general. The self-was invisible. His body was part of him, but not him as the real him was perceived from his mind. So, he was Spirit, first and not body. He was something different, and he felt it from within his spirit.

Ben discovered another dimension of self, different from what he could touch or see. He discovered his mind, which from this day onwards would command his existence. This was the centre of every decision he made. He was now conscious of his being, his individuality his existence, and his relationship to his surroundings. The discovery of self and the other was a complex development as the other was at the same time different from him though like him. In Platonist terms, "the other interweaves the same" and Descartes asserts that the act of consciousness becomes a substance which grasps its pure being in the act of the "cogito", a thoughts process. Meaning that one cannot be without his thoughts. Descartes suggests that essentially my nature is to think. "I think, therefore, I am"

This goes for everything that exists. hence, for a car to be, the concept first starts from the thought-the mind of his inceptor, and any physical manifestation is via this a thought process without which we cannot make it. Any process of building such will follow the concept perceived through the act of thinking- reasoning. Man, thus becomes a thinking being due to his minds' ability, without which it is difficult to justify his existence. Transforming his environment or improving his life starts from a thought process.

This mental shift thus enabled Ben to perceive that he was different from others. He could distinguish between good choices and bad choices, make a difference between important things and trivial ones. Most importantly, he was singularly an individual, and potentially master of his life and his destiny. After all, if he had just decided to run, he would run. He could just choose to shout, and shouting would follow. Similarly, he could apply the same principle in every area of his life.

Ben was now, himself, a subject, perhaps object of his thoughts and free. He was ponderous!

As he pondered, he looked up. A vast and unending blue curtain, pierced with a round and glowing orb firing down shining rays, and sending tropical waves of heat throughout the village. It was the sun. Was it how the world was? How big was it? Ben's mind was troubled and marvelled.

Was the horizon beyond the village the end of the world? Was the whole world like this flat and almost desolate place? How and who created all of this? Ben was lost in imagination, and pondered even more as to whether he was living a dream or reality? In a blink of an eye, his entire universe had changed; his perspective of self and the world had changed. He was afraid, terrified as he started to understand the depth of what he had just discovered.

His mind was at work, and he continued to think and lost in his conjecture for hours, somehow locked in, with this unique, invisible, untouchable, but real to experience which was as vivid as ever. No one else could feel or live the experience in the same way he was. Some of the feelings were difficult to share as words were insufficient to explain them.

He imagined all sorts of good things: food, cars, aeroplanes, ships, big cities, flourishing farms, lots of animals, both domestic and wild, the bush, a forest with all sorts of trees, and a vast and unending sea. He imagined himself in a big house, eating the best meal and in the company of beautiful people and the prettiest wife. He envisioned employing servants in a castle he had just built. He, in his head, had grown up living an ideal life. He imagined the most beautiful and fulfilled life that could cross his mind. He imagined writing books to share his experiences with the world. He imagined a different market square, painted without mud when it rains. He imagined beautiful buildings and skyscrapers rising in an imaginary city in his country.

Ben imagined well-built roads that led to the village and beyond. It was so beautiful and real that he could not tell if he was living this reality or if it was a dream. Ben concluded without a doubt that the images in his mind should exist somewhere and he therefore made up his mind experience and live in these delightful conditions one day. If he could perceive it, it was surely possible. So, he thought!

It was a tremendous experience, the most beautiful world in which he saw himself fulfilled. As he enjoyed this imaginary experience, he began to think about his immediate environment. It was not as wonderful and fulfilling as the picture he had in his imagination. For example, there were some experiences that he preferred to get rid of. Those related to his family's deprivation. He wanted to see his mum working less but eating the kinds of beautiful meals he had imagined. He wanted to buy machines so that his mum and dad could produce more with fewer efforts.

He imagined perfect weather; not too hot, not too cold, and went as far as thinking about an instrument to make this a reality. He imagined himself living in a house where the temperature was just right; he imagined working on the streets with no mud or excessive heat.

Moving on, he scanned his village and dreamed of better conditions, snow- capped mountains, a lush forest filled with palms, and tree ferns growing along the forest floor with various coloured orchids would grow in the forest. A stream running along the valley with beautiful rivers flowing gently to the middle of a vast paddy field. The chattering of birds with mellow sound. This imagination of natural scenery that could really imbued Ben with an incredible feeling.

Ben came back to his senses when he was troubled by his sister's piercing cries. She was hungry and had been crying for nearly an hour. Lost in his conjecture, Ben had failed to notice his sister. Now, awaken by her loud cries, he returned to reality that he now hated. He had tasted the world, beautiful beyond comprehension, and he was convinced this could exist somewhere. He could also create what he saw in his spirit. He was convinced that there could be a better world than the one in which he was living. He was convinced that all he had captured in his mind could become a reality, touchable and liveable.

Now, aware of the power within, Ben decided to dedicate his life in search of better living conditions. To pursuit a life where he could be happy and fulfilled. He declared aloud that he would live his mind's reality, rather than settling with what his environment provided. Without being told by anyone, he became convinced that through his mind, through the power of his thoughts he could make the world better.

He had clearly understood that his spiritual, mental, and psychological conditions would determine his physical reality. That the quality of his mind would determine his future. That the quality of his mind would determine his wealth and determine where he lived, what he did, how he behaved, what he said, what he had, who he dealt with, where he went and how his life would be. His mind would define who he would be.

His mind was, therefore, the key to his true self. He wasn't without his mind, and he couldn't be said to be fully human and conscious without his mind. Though the new world he had discovered was not materially in existence in Mengang, he perceived that what he saw in his spirit could become a reality, if he worked at making this happen. He could make it happen. He perceived that he could build skyscrapers, roads, better housing, improve the farming and transform the world. He had found his life purpose: He would dedicate the rest of his life to the pursuit of his dream.

As he made this decision, his sister's cries became louder. It was only a dream! He came back to his senses and attended to his sister.

After feeding his sister, Ben returned to work, or rather to his thoughts and dreams. These thoughts occupied his mind day and night. Ben would not let go, to the point that they started moulding his destiny. As he continued his quest for a better world, he continued to be convinced that his life's experience was only the outward expression of a reality that existed somewhere which could be found. Even as young as he was, he was determined to reject any thoughts that would hinder his willingness to succeed. He had chosen the sort of ideas that he would entertain going forward. Positive thoughts. Despite what was taking place in Mengang, he would entertain only positive thoughts.

Ben was developing an achiever's mentality; a state of mind that all Africans and all human beings in general should have. A positive thinking mind. He had turned a passive mindset to an active mindset. He would now search for solutions inwardly rather than from external sources. With this change of mindset, he was on the only sure path to changing his fortune. He was full of hope; he thought that life would be just as smooth as he pictured it being. Though this was true, he had not yet learned that despite being a spiritual being, he was living in a physical world. This meant he had to brave some challenges, perhaps the toughest challenges of all. Before achieving his goals and dreams. All successful people go through these tests; perhaps greater challenges signalled a brighter future.

Chapter 3

Rising Strong After a Fall

Ben was the son of Sekou. Sekou was born in Melong, grew up and worked there for some time before immigrating to Mengang later in his life. Sekou's father, Abada, was born in Saa'Nzok, however, in his youth, he moved to Nkong in search of a better life. After working as a sand carrier and on people's farms for years, he had nothing to show for his efforts. When he heard that something was happening in Melong, he moved there in search of a job. In this small town of Melong, new roads were being built by the government. The first road led to Mboroukou in the west and the second to a sea-town near Worri in the south via Barre.

Abada was told that road building jobs attracted better pay than any other employment that was on offer to the unqualified labour force. So, full of hope, he moved to Melong with his wife and their first two daughters. When he arrived in Melong, he was recruited by the road building contractor, thus achieving his dream. He was now earning more than he ever had before and the consistency of income started to improve their lives.

After few years in Melong, Abada had a son, and he was joyous. He named him Sekou. However, after the birth of Sekou, Abada and his wife tried to have more children in vain. So Sekou was the only male amongst two older siblings.

Abada's wife complemented the family income by working on the farm, and they were a happy family; unfortunately, this happy life changed when Abada suddenly died in a road building accident.

One day, as they were digging, there was a landslide, which covered Abada. The amount of soil that fell on him was so huge that after days of digging and searching, they could not find his body. So, no one knew exactly where his body was and without the body, it was hard to mark a spot as his grave. To date, there was no marked grave for

Abada. Henceforth, up till now, it was hard for his descendants to know how old he was when he died. His date of birth was unknown. His real age was only a guess, and the memory of his life remained only with his wife and children.

Abada's death had little impact on the company and was barely noticed by his bosses, and the work continued as if nothing had happened. Conversely, this loss was devastating for his family. They grieved for weeks; the absence of his body only added to their misery. About two months after his father's death, Sekou, who was only 13, approached the clerk of the road building company for employment. To show their sympathy towards the family, they employed him as a child labourer.

Securing employment was a limelight for the household because Sekou's small salary helped for the family's upkeep, and most importantly, the family was happy because, for them, it was an achievement. For Sekou, this was far from an achievement; in his mind, he wanted to study like children of his age, play on the street with friends; working at this early age was more of a burden than freedom. Henceforth, he was on his way to perpetuating his father's poverty and misery, and perhaps, he could be buried alive like his father, and he disliked it. Nonetheless, he worked in Melong for 14 years before the completion of the roads.

Five years after Sekou started working, he got married at the age of 18 and had his first child at 19. Over a period of eight years, Sekou and his wife had five children. Ben was the third child, and at 27, Sekou had five children. By this time, the road works were completed, and Sekou found himself in a desperate situation as he became unemployed with no income.

Despite knowing when the road building was scheduled to complete, no worker was prepared for life post-road works.

After a few months without another job in Melong, Sekou decided to move to Mengang where he heard there was a prosperous market which attracted people from all four corners of the county. They first tested the market with the produce of their farm to make sure people could by them there. This experience was positive; however, this market was seven days walk from Melong and Sekou soon decided to move his family to Mengang.

After many months in Mengang, he managed to secure work on various farms and subsequently acquired his farm where his wife, Kristi, worked day and night tirelessly to feed their five children while Sekou was labouring in other people's farms to supplement their income.

Ben was just a few months away from his third birthday when they moved to Mengang, and he couldn't remember anything about Melong. Mengang was his world, his village, and possibly his future.

When he was not at school, he was either helping on the farm or looking after his siblings. A few years after settling in Mengang, Sekou, who had learned to work hard from the age of 13, started to thrive in Mengang because he accepted most of the jobs that most people from the village despised. He was mocked and ridiculed by villagers, but he did not mind. The most important thing for him was to feed his family.

Through dedication, focus and hard work, he soon started to make more money than anyone else in the village. With the money earned from his labour, he bought cattle, sheep and chicken and grew produce, which he sold. By the time Ben was nine, Sekou had become a trader and regarded as one of the richest people in Mengang. In only six years after settling in Mengang, Sekou had made tremendous progress thanks to his hard work, dedication, focus, insightful vision, and careful planning. He knew why he came to Mengang and he never lost focus on what was important to him; succeeding and living a comfortable life with his family was his priority and his vision was to leave a lasting legacy to all those who would ever bear his name.

Envious and jealous of Sekou's success, the villagers gathered and plotted to force him to depart from Mengang. They couldn't believe that a foreigner, who, just six years earlier, came empty handed, living on handouts with his family; a foreigner who was given a plot of land at a very low price, a foreigner who, just a few years ago was being mocked because he accepted any job that came his way, a foreigner who was not as strong or as handsome as other people in the village was making a fortune in a relatively short time in a village where the majority of its inhabitants were poor.

To force him out of the village, they labelled him a wizard, then decided to expel the so-called sorcerer from their village. They planned this secretly for months without Sekou's knowledge. One morning at around 6AM, when Sekou, Kristi, and their children had just woken up and were preparing for their daily routine, their life took an unexpected turn.

As always, Ben had already had his shower and was getting ready for school. Kristi was shouting at Mamie, her youngest daughter, urging her to wake up and prepare for school, while Sekou was in the kitchen fetching what to eat before making his usual morning tour, which typically involved checking his cattle, pigs and chicken. From the kitchen, Sekou heard a loud bang on his door. The knock was very loud. It was immediately apparent that something was wrong, but what could it be? Who had died in the village? The news of the death was one of the only reasons someone would knock at this time of the day with such intensity. In any case, Sekou anticipated bad news as he proceeded to open the door.

As he prepared to open the door, he heard many voices urging him and his family to come out quickly or risk being burned alive in the house. People were calling him names, chanting and cursing his whole family. By the time he opened the door, he knew that their lives were in danger, and, as soon as the door was opened, people entered the house in masses and started scattering their stuff before evicting them from their home and from the village. Sekou and his family were gripped with fear and in shock because they didn't know why they were being treated so harshly.

It was an incredible scene of cruelty and violence, as the whole village had gathered in front of their house urging them to leave the village immediately. They were not allowed to take any of their possessions. The villagers claimed they were wizards and that their belongings, including their house, would be confiscated.

When Sekou tried to resist, but the villagers rushed toward him and dragged him away. Unable to overcome the weight crushing him down, he gave up, and they were dragged away into the bushes nearby and ordered to leave without looking back. The only place they could settle was the forest of Zibing, a borderland unclaimed by any of the two neighbouring villages. Zibing was a dense fearsome forest called a "Cursed Forest".

Crying with all their strength, Sekou and his entire family ran for their lives into this fearsome forest in which no villager had ever dared to venture in. People imagined all sorts of animals living in it. They believed that whoever entered the forest would die. By ordering Sekou and his family to settle into this forest, their enemies were confident that they would not survive.

In addition to stealing their house and sharing all their possessions, the people of Mengang forbade Sekou from ever coming back to the village for any reason.

As they cried, they proceeded deeper and deeper into the forest, stumbling on tree trunks. Still crying they continued blindly through the dense, dark forest. The density of the forest made it difficult for the daylight to penetrate the forest, particularly at this early hour of the day. So, still moving forward without knowing where they were going, they could only see a faint glow of light through the dense and gloomy leaves.

As they continued, their nostrils were filled with dampness. They smelt the muggy earth that squelched beneath their feet. They tread lightly, fearful of the many spooky and mysterious noises that come from all directions. Nonetheless, they hesitantly advanced, though gripped with fear. Suddenly something big and dark flapped across their path, escalating their anxiety. They quickly discovered it was only an owl. This big old owl proceeded to sit on a high branch, cooing loudly as if to warn others of Sekou and his family's humble presence in this unconquered wilderness. Undeterred by the cooing noises of the lonely owl, Sekou and his family continued their way until they were far from any recognisable trail, deeper into the heart of the forest.

By this time, they began to bushwhack, their legs burning from the poisonous plants. Gathering their strength, they trekked another mile or so at a steep incline until they didn't think they could take another step. There was no end in sight. Sekou decided the next direction they would take. As fate would have it, the weather started giving some warning signs. With a leap of faith which felt like jumping off a cliff, they began to zoom toward the deepest west side of the forest.

When they encountered a fierce breeze, Sekou knew they would soon face rain. They quickened as if they were heading to a refuge. In fact, it was their human instinct reacting out of self-preservation. They continued walking as the clouds gathered in the sky which, up to then had been a perfect plasma-blue with no indication that sudden changes were about to take place. Before this abrupt change, the clouds had looked like airy anvils drifting under the twinkling waves that filtered through the dense forest, but now was beginning to darken even more in this already sombre vegetation. They nonetheless reached a less dense part of the forest, and what they could see were large pillows of cloud that were forming, blotting out the golden sun that had just started to rise.

The first splatter of rain began to melt on them, as they advanced further into the depth of the forest, still without any definite destination in mind. They continued and soon entered an Amazonian-like part of the forest and took shelter under an old oak tree, hoping that they could see out the shower. Droplets of moisture began to drip from the leaves and drained down right on their heads. They had given up the fight to stay away from the rain.

As if losing their home was not enough, they were now in the middle of a torrential downpour. A wall of rain drenched the oak tree; the drops were drumming against the canopy with a rhythm; it reminded them that nothing, but misery lay ahead. As they proceeded, Ben had a flashback to his dream that he had on the market day. Was it going to happen one day? He rejected any thoughts that suggested that his dream was impossible or would be halted by this new adventure.

So much rain was falling that the sound blurred into one long, whirring noise like the rotor blades of a helicopter. This went on for hours. When the noise level eventfully started to lessen, the drops faded into a musical chime.

Neither Sekou, his wife nor any of his children had ever experienced such intense rainfall. Perhaps it was because they usually escaped into a house somewhere before it got worse. On this occasion, they had no choice but to endure the rain to the brink as there was no house close by, and, even if there were, they wouldn't dare to approach it, considering the severe warning they were given when being forcefully evicted from their home for no real reason except envy.

They were now deep into the forest and uncertain of their future, and the rain continued until late. By the time the rain ended, night had started falling.

Up, the moon seemed to turn the leaves into a flaming patchwork of colours: scorching yellows, lava reds and burnished browns. As they sat under the oak tree, they could see a greedy thrush finishing a snail by tapping it on a rock and then finishing his supper with a song of triumph before fluttering away.

The mournful cry of a lone fox echoed through the vault-still silence of the trees as a huffing wind rose, stirring the flaps of the oak leaves causing a fluttering noise that pierced their hearts. They all trembled at once, before realising that it was nothing dangerous. Once more, the remaining bouts of rainwater and thumping balloons of sopping moisture felt on them, they trembled again and again until they became used to this scene.

They had been crying the whole day and the downpour had given them a shower and rid their faces from the marks of tears that would have otherwise remained for days. Everyone had forgotten about food as if hunger was non-existent. Despite being distressed, Sekou found the strength to appease his wife and children. He reassured them that all would be okay, though they had no roof over their head and had not eaten the whole day. Worse than that, they had no home to go to, and nothing else in the world, to reassure them of a possible stable future. They were going to spend the night in the middle of the forest. Perhaps, they stood no chance of seeing the next day. By this time, the day was already very advanced. It was hard to imagine that they were already in the night.

During this early part of the night, Sekou gathered the strength to hunt rats. He caught two and cooked them on a pile of wood with fruits picked by Kristi. That was their combined breakfast, dinner, and supper. Sekou always carried a lighter and a small knife called a pan-knife; these were the only tools they had at their disposal to survive.

After eating, they cut some grass to make a bed under a tall tree as they prepared to spend their first night in the open. The children were tired, and with their parents on their side, they cared less about whether they were in the forest or at home;

soon they fell asleep one by one. Sekou and his wife played the sentinels until their strength started giving up. They had no plan, not for the night nor the next day.

As Sekou slept, he unconsciously was determined to brave the situation and to emerge as from it a man. He had been a man since the age of 13 and this test was not going to bring him down. He reflected on what his dad once told him: that he was made in God's image, he was God-like and God's son, as such, he was able to do all things. While he did not have the chance to spend many years with his dad, some of his good advice still resonated in his mind particularly in difficult times.

In the middle of the night, a huffing wind stirred the flaps of the oak trees under which they were camping. They had no choice but to endure it, at least for that night. The night was short, perhaps because they were exhausted and had a deep sleep.

At dawn, Sekou saw, just meters away from where they spent their night, a tall baobab that they used to see far away from the village. This giant baobab was in the thick forest of Zibing. He remembered that they were in the cursed forest of Zibing, the only place they could settle in. People thought that Zibing forest was sacred and considered anyone who entered that forest as either witch or God. In fact, they believed that no human being could survive in this forest.

He had heard stories about this place but had never been near since he settled in Mengang. He vividly remembered people saying that anyone who entered this forest died, but he was convinced that neither himself nor any member of his family would perish in this forest. His conviction became even stronger as they survived the first night as he realised that this forest was no different from any other woodland. No one was in agony, and their immediate concerns was to make a shelter for themselves.

Sekou was convinced that all the stories he had heard about the forest was a fallacy. If no one had ever entered the forest, how did they know that they couldn't survive in it? Henceforth, if he was made in God's image, then he was a god and had every right to be there. He had no choice because he had no other place to go to. It did not even cross his mind to return to Melong, where he lived until he was 27, or go to his ancestor's land in Saa' Nzock.

Since he had already entered god's sacred forest, he could only wait for the sentence.

Every time he pondered over the villagers' stories about this forest, he was reassured when he remembered that he was overcome every adversity. Once he had this revelation all fears left him, and he became increasingly confident that he could draw on a solution from heaven.

He looked up and tuned in for answers. He started wandering in the wild in search of nothing in particular. This ballad in the middle of nowhere helped him to gather his thoughts to find a way to make the best out of this situation. He could learn from every experience, irrespective of whether it was bad or good. As the Bible says, all things work for good for those who believe and love God, and who are called according to his purpose. If he was the temple of the Holy Spirit, the Spirit of the all-knowing, powerful God, a solution was certainly not far away. Where could he go? He was confident that he and his family would survive. In fact, he had no choice; he had to survive. He was now determined to do something that he had never done before: building a new home in the middle of the forest with practically no tools.

He was a bit wet, having walked through the moistened grass that had retained water from the rain. He saw from afar a small stream falling from the hill and walked towards it. As he took a step closer, goose bumps dashed up to his spine. His body was shivering as if he was in a freezer. The trees were waving at him as he took a few more steps through the animal path as the wind ran aggressively through the wrinkly, naked, brown branches. He proceeded, not without difficulties, through the ocean of thorn grasses that abounded in this spot.

The cold air sunk half of his brown dead body like a lion eating its prey. The trees swayed back and forth trying to look for breathing space. The foggy mist made it impossible to see in the near distance. The power of the sun penetrated the fog and unleashed the happier side of the forest. The shimmering arc filtered through the sky and a rainbow reflected its beauty above the forest.

He heard a voice behind him say, "Never before have I seen this limelight. How beautiful. I could hear the calming chirps of the birds slowly making my dream and almost putting me to sleep.

The aggressive strength of the wild reveals the might of God. I am thrilled! I like it here!".

Sekou trembled and turned quickly to look. It was Ben, his son, his dreamer, his philosopher, the positive one who always saw good in everything. But it was perhaps a bit much today. How could he be painting such a beautiful picture of nature in this time of trouble? Didn't he know what they were going through? He refrained from rebuking him and invited him to come closer, and they both stood side by side, looking at the waterfall.

They stood for a long while without exchanging a word. Eventually, they started to talk. They were focussed on one thing: How to make their lives better as they began to put their ideas together on how to make a shelter for themselves and how to survive in the forest. They decided there and then that they were not moving any further. This would become their home and their new village. They would do what it took to survive, and they had no choice but to win. After all, they had survived their first night without any hiccups; so, could it be for the second, the third, the fourth and the rest of their days and nights in the so-called sacred forest of Zibing - the much talked-about forest. No one had dared to enter the forest as they feared they would die.

Once people knew that they had gone into the forest, they assumed that they would die for sure, and so, were classified as dead.

Meanwhile, Sekou used dead wood and battled for hours to cut some sticks that he used to make a hut. It took days, but they finally constructed a shelter. They started using any tools they found to hunt and plant a garden. Sekou seized this as an opportunity to meditate and executed good ideas that came to his mind.

Drawing from his experience in Mengang, Sekou was determined to make an impact. Now he had found an ally in his son Ben. He figured out that, if he was able to make a fortune in Mengang after arriving with nothing, he was able to make a fortune anywhere. He was convinced that success was not confined to a place, rather it was a state of mind. He urged his family to put their minds to work. They found old objects like very old machetes in the forest. These objects were carried into the forest by the torrential rains or left behind by those lost who courage to venture into the forest. Despite their fragility, the old tools helped to make their lives better.

No individual or village had never claimed the land. Fortunately, as its first inhabitants, Sekou claimed the land for his family by right. They did as much as they could with the land. Still putting their minds to work, they improved their shelter. In the beginning, when people saw the smoke in the middle of the forest, they became even more afraid of the forest. No one could imagine that people had settled in, and the smoke that came out of their shelter whether by night or day terrified the inhabitants in the neighbouring villages. It took many years for people to realise that some people may have settled in the forest, but no one knew who the settlers were, and no one dared to enter the forest. One day, Sekou took his courage to go all the way closer to the path that led to Letieu, a village close by. He related his story to people and word soon spread around, and it is at this time that he began bartering with people living nearby. Word spread out, and soon people started coming from other villages to exchange goods that Sekou needed, such as tools and domestic animals, for game meat and delicious fruits from the forest.

Still, no one dared to enter the forest. This isolation and quietness were a unique opportunity for Sekou and his family to work hard and to think creatively. They had to use their mind and the power of their imagination to make the most of their time in the wild. This was paying off when people began to trade with them.

The tools that they received in exchange for their produce enabled Sekou to try new techniques for growing his crops. They had nothing else to do apart from working and reflecting on better ways to improve their lives. They were brilliant, and at some point, they acquired horses and donkeys and managed to tame the elephant. They used these animals for large agriculture programmes. In a short while, they were able to produce on an industrial scale.

Having been forbidden to go back to Mengang, Sekou could not sell his produce in that market, and for some time, they were limited to bartering. In exchange for his goods, he received sheep, chicken, swans, and cattle, - which he bred in the forest. And before long, he had livestock. And by the time people started to show interest in the forest, they had claimed the whole land. It was a vast area covering hundreds of thousands of acres. He renamed the land after himself. After seven years in the forest, Sekou was back on his feet with more land than anyone had ever had in his family.

He had become autonomous in a foreign land. No one dared to fight him because he was a god on account of his ability to enter a sacred forest and survive. As soon as the people from Mengang learned that he was alive and was doing well in Zibing, they called him a wizard. This myth around him, coupled with the mystery surrounding his background and family history, made people fear him even more; he became an undisputed owner of the land and the king of this forest he had just renamed Sekou.

Because he sold his produce cheaper than anyone else in the whole region, he attracted customers from the entire county and beyond. In the absence of money, he could accept anything as a means of payment. This new way of doing business attracted customers from many places, and he became comparable to a wholesaler from whom some people bought what they sold in Mengang market.

As his business continued to flourish in this once abandoned, and considered as cursed forest, people overcame the myth and fear of the forest. They understood that their fear of the woods was unjustified. As people continued to come, Sekou started building shops and employing helpers to sell for him so he could focus on other things.

He made hundreds of stores to meet the growing demand for his goods. Also, he built houses where his workers stayed and then progressively started renting some and using others as guesthouses. People soon began to queue to work for him. Zibing, renamed Sekou, had become a more desirable environment to live in. It was growing in reputation; its market had now overtaken Mengang's market, and Sekou continued to build more houses.

From a desolate forest, Sekou became a village, then a city. A city that sprang out of the forest in the middle of nowhere. In less than 20 years, Sekou had developed into a place where everyone wanted to live. From misfortune to glory, from disgrace to fortune, Sekou founded a city which now bore his name, and which became notable in the whole country.

He had proven that poverty was more of a state of mind and that any place could be transformed to a thriving, rich and attractive location if its inhabitants had a rich and creative mind. A poor man is the one who has lost his mind, not the one who has lost his fortune. He had understood that one's mind determines his possessions and his position.

He who loses his mind loses his fortune and his future. He who loses his mind is worthless. But if you lose all material things with your mind intact, you can rebuild your wealth. He who can make good use of his mind can change the world. If you can think well enough, you can find a solution for every single problem. He who makes good use of his mind can change the course of history. Your mind will determine your position in society and the level of responsibility you are given. Therefore decision makers in any company or government department work less but earn more than anyone else. People trust their judgement and decision-making abilities. They trust their wisdom.

This was a lesson that Sekou was determined to pass on to his children. Unbeknownst to him, his son Ben had since the age of 9 understood these

POOR LAND OR POOR MINDS

principles and his father's exploits convinced him even more that his dream was not a nightmare, but something he could use to change his life.

He had seen his dad go from broke to blessed, homeless to a great landowner, from being exiled from a village to becoming a city king. Ben understood that all real advancements come from personal efforts, starting with a change of mindset, and a firm belief in one's abilities. Genuine and lasting change starts with a refusal to give up, backed up with great ideas, not per chance or by surprise.

A man, by his supreme efforts and through his will, may change his whole life and accomplish miracles. Anyone could be that man; everyone could be his Sekou - that a man with an unquenchable will can achieve whatever he desires. Human beings are interdependent and for this reason, they should help each other. Sekou's experience was a live example of this theory because by helping themselves, they were able to help the whole community and created a city out of the forest. However, this principle could only work when each of us did as he is supposed to. Successful people's stories should inspire and help us to adopt behavioural patterns that led them to accomplish greater things.

We cannot remain the same and be happy; we cannot remain the same and make an impact, we cannot remain the same and be rich. If we fail to change, we will not progress. As a result, we will continue to be impoverished.

Mengang had stayed the same, and its status quo created a spirit of jealousy; people came to believe that those who succeed in this village were infringing on their ability to thrive. It was not the case. One's ability to achieve does not limit the other's if each is innovative and creative. People say that birds don't collide in the sky because there is more than enough space for each one of them. So is the earth for humans. History reveals that one discovery had led to further development and innovation in different fields by people who had never collaborated or communicated before. This is what brings progress and increases prosperity for all.

If human beings remain the same, they will be missing the mark, and will not accomplish their mission on earth. The power of our thoughts commands us to think, change and produce continuously. This is how we can glorify God. If we are made in the image of God, we should always be working, without ever giving up. We should take our destiny in our hands and assume that no one else can come to the rescue. If our future matters to us, we should work on it as nothing else matters.

Sekou's future and his entire families depended on their willingness to preserve their lives; they survived and thrived in an unconquered forest. Knowingly or not, they understood the principle of success and the need to look forward, rather than remaining anchored by the past. They learned from their past and moved on to bigger challenges. This should be rooted in each person's passion for improvement.

One should keep his sense of purpose or direction in a crisis, as Sekou did while in the wild, and by acting in the same way, we create a real compass setting for those around to follow. It is possible to rely on other people to get the dream off the ground, but others can only be a source of inspiration, as each holds the key to open their door to success.

It is important to constantly look inwardly to find the solutions, while leveraging our current assets, owning our mistakes and immediately thinking of ways to improve next time, to ensure the same mistakes are not repeated. Success is something that all of us wish to attain. It is also an easy thing to achieve but only if we want it. Unfortunately, few people are so completely willing to make it their number one focus and priority. This explains why success is exclusive to a handful of individuals who do extraordinary things.

Being successful is all about how badly you want it and how much you are willing to work for it, no matter where you are and despite all the setbacks.

Out of necessity, Sekou created a whole city in the middle of a forest. Most people would have given up. Some people may have taken their own lives away or left their families and ran away from their responsibilities. Other people may have chosen to migrate yet again to another corner of the country, but Sekou didn't. He faced the situation, confronted the difficulties, and won. He now has a city bearing his name. Who would have thought an orphan, exploited through child labour from the age of 13, with no father around to guide him would have ended up being a leader and king in a foreign land? Sekou's life principle forged his destiny.

There was always a leader inside of him, only he did not know it. In every human being, there is a potential inventor, a visionary, a great leader, and a trendsetter for a generation. The circumstances leading to success and achievement may be unplanned, but one must be prepared to embrace and make the most of these conditions.

There are millions of people scratching the surface despite living in gold mines. There are millions of people hunting for rats while residing in the richest forests in the world; they will eventually be removed by force to less fruitful areas of the land by those who are seeking to acquire their land to exploit its resources. It is not so much about how much money one can invest to achieve their dreams; it is a matter of determination and focus. Those who do not know what they are looking for will come across a diamond and toss it away, but those who can see the beauty in it will use it to their advantage.

Millions of people, if not billions, achieve less than their fathers or mothers. Millions of people waste their lives just because dad or mum made it, and they can get away with doing very little. They think they are lucky. However, they ignore the fact that they are living on their parents' achievements.

Mum or dad may have achieved a lot, but each child has his purpose, which a life of self-gratification cannot unveil. It is only through an endless search for meaning that one can make an impact in the world and make a difference to the lives of billions of people. The determination to achieve and overcome obstacles is at the heart of great achievements and discoveries.

Living on other people's achievements is akin to living other people's lives. Living on other people's dreams and successes is living a borrowed life. Ben had a choice: he could live on his dad's achievement or find his purpose. He was neither stupid nor lazy and was not afraid of what people would say if he failed. Ben was not concerned about millions of eyes looking at him. He was not mindful about potential hindrances ahead. He knew only one thing: he was not satisfied and had not achieved any of his dreams. There is no age limit to make it. At any time, at any age, one can decide to change the course of his life. Ben was ready to pursue his dreams. He had a will of steel.

Ben had made his plans and informed his family. He was leaving Sekou to chase his dream.

Chapter 4

A Dream Chaser

At 30, Ben had not completed his secondary education, nor accomplished any of the many dreams he had as a child. As a child, he had dreamed of completing his A levels at 17 and starting his own business.

Since his childhood, he had dreamed of becoming the richest person in his country by the age of 60. But due to hindrances he had in his childhood, had not built his dream house, and neither had he transformed Mengang as he wished by 30 as he planned. He had always wanted to build schools and to live in a mansion. He wanted to own all sorts of animals. He had dreamed of living on an island and owning helicopters and jet planes.

He had dreamed of travelling the world and helping people. Most importantly he had dreamed of letting the world know that all things were possible, and that man was the only one who could decide the limits of his achievements. He wanted to convey this message to others to encourage millions of people like him, who were languishing in a sea of poverty. But he couldn't do this when he had nothing to show for it. The only way he could help and encourage others was first to achieve his dreams. At 30, it was not too late he said to himself and he made up his mind to do it, no matter what it took.

Despite being rejected and excluded from Mengang, all his childhood dreams started there, and he cherished that place more than the city built by his dad. He believed in humans' limitless possibilities. What he saw in his spirit as a child was still vivid and stirring up his anger for accomplishment.

His ambitions of becoming one of the world's great achievers had not died despite his age. He decided to go back to school. He had never completed his GCSEs. However, he understood that when a man loses his grip or control on certain aspects of his life, he must win his redemption by his own will. He didn't have any choice or power over what happened to them in Mengang, but now he had a choice as to how he wanted to live his life, and how to make it count. It was a personal affair. Though he needed encouragement and advice from friends, mentors or family members, his ability to regain the right road remained an intimate affair.

At 30 Ben was convinced that even if he had a lifespan of 50 years, he had another 20 years to achieve his dream. He went as far as thinking that, if he were to leave the earth at 35 or 40, he would have started to fulfil part of his dream. It was his duty. None else was like him. no one else could fulfil his purpose on his behalf; therefore, he needed to concentrate all his energies and attention on achieving his goals.

Ben's dad did not receive anyone's help when they were forced into the forest from where they rebuilt their lives from scratch. This reassured him that he was also able to achieve great things. In the wilderness, Sekou's willingness to live stirred his resolve to conquer hardship and his potential weaknesses. Understanding that no one could do it for him, he kept pressing demand upon his mind for solutions. This was a valuable lesson for his son who was resolute to leave his mark on earth. He wanted to make his life meaningful. He knew that he would have an easy ride if he stayed in Sekou where he was now well-known. If he chose to study there, the teachers would be lenient toward him. He had to move away from his family. Despite moving toward uncertainty, he remained resolute to achieve his dreams. Schooling was only a starting point. After his A-levels, he intended to progress toward his big projects. Ben was neither ashamed nor afraid to start afresh.

He wanted to go far beyond his father's achievement. His father was a local hero; Ben was dreaming of becoming an international star. He was not scared of difficulties, and his motto was: "Anything that requires only a small effort, makes skinny use of one's abilities". What requires fewer efforts, or only a tiny proportion of our abilities, yields a little harvest of achievement. A single effort from an individual can transform the world, even though success does not come cheap. Great success requires a lot of effort and perseverance. The bigger a dream, the tougher the challenges.

Ben knew that perseverance was the price to pay for his big ideas. Yes, the price was not so much in money, but in effort and determination, underpinned by a desire to do what was required. Individual progress, achievement and success come from personal efforts.

Efforts cannot be made on a void. Genuine efforts must be aimed at achieving a planned goal. But was it not too late at 30 to return to school for a GCSE and to attempt his A level at possibly 32? Nothing was too far from his reach, and the time it could take to achieve his dream didn't matter.

Before dawn on the 1st of February, Ben left Sekou to unknown territories. He only had enough provisions for few days and just enough money for few weeks. Nonetheless, he wanted to go as far as he could. On his first day, he walked 30 miles through a small path in the forest and decided to spend his first night in the open. When night emerged, and as darkness advanced, questions began to trouble his mind: "why did you leave a comfortable life to venture into the unknown"? "What if this dream never happens"? "Why go back to school at 30"? As he continued to ponder, he became exhausted and soon fell asleep. When he woke up in the middle of the night, he was surrounded by a brief silence; but not for long because he soon realised that all sorts of creatures that love the night world were extremely active around him. The forest was full of spooky noises. Breaking through this noise was another more reassuring noise from far away; it was the sound of native drums piercing through the night from a neighbouring village. Despite being from afar, the drums sounded as if they were close by. Ben remained awake for some time. He wanted to walk all the way to the village, but he quickly abandoned the idea as he realised, he could be recognised in the community and perhaps convinced by someone to return home. He didn't want to take the risk or give up so soon. They spent a year in the forest, and nothing ever happened to them. He was only about 30 miles from his village and wanted to avoid settling anywhere he would enjoy favour or preferential treatment. If he were to be recognised, he was sure they would assist him. He wanted to move to a place where he would be anonymous and treated like any other person. As the minutes slipped by, the sound seemed to come nearer and nearer. By this time, it was becoming colder, and his tension mounted rapidly. He tried to focus on his dream instead of accommodating the negative thoughts that were susceptible of convincing him to return home.

Thoughts are like a double-edged sword. They can build or destroy your dream. Ben preferred to entertain constructive thoughts instead. He opted to follow encouraging rather than discouraging thoughts. When Ben remembered vividly how his family had slept in the open in a more frightful forest one year, he became more determined to chase his dream. He now considered the noises around him a regular part of life; if there were ever anything threatening, he would face it and win. With this determination, he got back to sleep.

The next day, he woke up early and headed North West for another 47 miles and spent another night at the foot of the high mountains of Coupé. The third day he advanced for another 40 kilometres. He finally reached his randomly selected destination after eight days, having covered 290 miles. By this time, he had reached a small remote village called Leke.

He was exhausted and almost close to death with sores all over his feet. It would take him weeks to recover. In this unknown village, he had to negotiate a place to stay. He had nothing left to eat and just a little bit of money. He wondered around the village square in search of a host.

Leke was a tiny camping area with only a handful of inhabitants; the new town- the centre- was not far away with a calm, unhurried air on this blustery weekday afternoon. Scarcely populated, Leke was like a desolate land with only paths and huts surrounded by subsistence farming. From afar, Ben saw some domestic animals and children playing on the street. The village had many paths leading to houses. Close to where the children were playing was a larger path leading a to the main road which prolonged all the way to the city.

As he proceeded towards the children, Ben met a young man in gumboots herding sheep. He greeted the shepherd. He was the only young adult he had met so far. People appeared to work on their farms hidden behind the forest or mountains around the village. It was not hot; however, the air was thick with the smell of damp, mixed with fresh seaweed. This scent was probably caused by animal droppings. The village was made up of about two dozen houses, mainly huts. Due to the sun, they were silhouetted against fields of peat, coloured in soft yellows, browns and greens. In the near distance was a disputed area that Ben would soon discover was called Tsang. Tsang was just a mile away and covered a large area which included the newly created city centre and beyond.

With a population barely in the three digits, Leke (pronounced "Lekeu") seemed like a world away from the glossy opulence of the capital. However, it was in this peaceful, uneven, mountainous, marshy, and extremely poor land that Ben chose to settle.

The villagers of Leke were considered among the most isolated and the most secluded in the whole country. They didn't know much about what was going on in the outside world. In this area surrounded by mountains, the weather was severe at times and was much colder than the rest of the country. Europeans who were making their first steps in the country quickly learned that Leke's climate was like theirs. So, they chose it for one of their military mission centres.

The villagers had been living in the area for over ten generations, but it still looked like a camping area. Every day villagers complained that the village could not meet their needs, even though they were surrounded by fertile lands, fresh waters, and a desirable landscape.

If this area was so poor, why were the Europeans coming there? What did they see in this village that the villagers themselves had not noticed? It was mind blowing. What attracted Ben to this remote place? Only time would tell.

Ben greeted the shepherd again.

"Are you from here?" the shepherd asked.

"No," Ben replied.

"I was wondering, because you don't look familiar".

"Yes, I wonder if you could help me. I would like to stay in this village for a while". "You are welcome, my brother. You are welcome to stay in our house. Here we do not reject strangers".

The conversation carried on. To his astonishment, Ben learned that his host was a married man with two children even though he was only 19 years old. His first child was 2 and the second one was about four months old. This meant that he got married at either 16 or 15. Ben was almost double his age but was still single and trying to achieve his dream. This young man, Babou, was living his life. What mattered to him was to eat, feed his family and procreate. He did not want anything other than to live, eat, and enjoy the pleasure of having a wife with whom he had children. Most people, if not everyone in this village behaved the same. As soon as a person reached puberty, he/she got married to someone from the same or a neighbouring village.

People did not have any ambition beyond their immediate needs for survival and mating. They ate what they grew as their ancestors did the same. Their houses were built in the same way as their forefathers' and had not changed for centuries.

Babou was just another person mimicking his ancestors. There was no fuss about thinking big or thinking outside of the box. In fact, no one cared or ventured into the unknown, and none thought that building more major roads or houses was important.

Ben moved in with his host Babou. Late that night, Mamou, Babou's wife, returned and greeted their host with joy. There were no questions about where he came from, his name, where he would sleep, or when he was planning on returning. Ben introduced himself to Mamou, but they decided to call him "Tan", which meant visitor in their local language.

Ben was unwell for his first week and could not walk but, as soon as he recovered, he started helping Babou with shepherding and farming. He also took any work he could find in the village to make some money. From his modest appearance, no one could have guessed the privileges he had left behind in Sekou in the pursuit of his dream.

When he had enough money for his tuition fee, he enrolled at the school and started studying for his GCSEs, which he passed. The next academic year he joined again for his pre-A Levels; after three years in Leke, he obtained his A Levels. Upon obtaining his A levels aged 33, he took on a job as a schoolteacher in Leke and nearby Tsang.

He continued to save money, and when he had enough, he bought a plot of land to build his own house. He complemented his income by working as a private tutor. He accepted food, goats, sheep, chicken, and anything that people could afford to give as means of payment. Learning from his dad, he practised bartering, which helped him to build up capital in livestock, goods, and money quickly.

In all his undertakings, Ben was extremely dedicated and supported hundreds of students to pass their exams. Bit by bit, he bought more land and ventured into a trade which he diversified.

Five years after his graduation, he managed to buy hectares of land in this village and soon acquired other acres of land in Tsang West, a disputed area between King Leke and King Foto. He managed to convince the people of Foto to sell what they claimed to be theirs and the people of Leke to sell the part they were claiming as their own and paid extra to settle the dispute between the two tribes and became the owner of a vast domain in Tsang. His progress was awesome and Babou, who was younger than him, did not understand how he could manage to become so great in a very short time, in a land that they thought was poor.

Ben tried to convince Babou to change the way he grew his crops and livestock, but he wouldn't listen; as he continued to do things the way he was used to, so his life remained the same. Ben now considered Babou as a family member and supported him and his family irrespective of whether they changed their ways or not. He made up his mind to rescue Babou's children from his backwards thinking and sent them to the best schools.

After acquiring his land in Tsang, he invited his dad to see it. This was Sekou's first visit to his son since he left home and his first in this part of the country.

The land Ben bought in Tsang was a place of astonishing beauty. Letieu and Fou with Ngwata in the south-west, Bale in the south, Fotetsa in the west and Bing in the east. The western area boasted two great lakes. The great lake was just at the foot of Mont Fotetsa, from where you could see mountains composed of granite and covered with thorny shrubs and acacia trees. These mountains thrust spires of naked rock into the heavens so high that you would believe the very sky was pierced. A forest stretched all the way to Ngwata. The river NKam led to Worri, which continued to the estuary of the Atlantic about 150 miles downstream. A beautiful valley led to the plain of Bono, bounded on three sides by basalt outcrops and partially screened by the brush. It followed the ridge down toward a patch of grass towards the surrounding village of Tough.

As the mist lifted, the dull patches of blue glowing far beyond the cliffs gradually came into view. The great lake was a vigorous and optimistic with blue-back and rotting logs that some long-forgotten flood had deposited crossways on the spit mouth of a thick sulphurous stream fed the great river of Nkam.

Great mudstone outcropped the banks of the Nkam, easing over humps and trenches, with potholes and stone rivers bashed through the trees where a track was blocked, and the bucking, climbing steep eroded banks at times caused landslides along the banks. There were occasional tufts of trees such as acacias and baobabs, and grasses and shrubs spread, on-again-off-again, as far as the eye could see. Atop the brown earthen crust, you could see a surface that looked as soft as freshly prepared land for crop growing, and somehow not less inviting.

In the surrounding forest, you could see a large outcropping of bundled roots from the remains of dead baobabs and Sapele trees that had broken free from the hard, packed, dense vegetation alongside the riverbanks. A bare Ebene tree that crossed the river's highway required downshifting to cross safely. The miles, the motion, the flat wide-open land, furnished with a dense forest here and there, the twisted Sapele trees, baobabs, acacias, and other exotic plants that grew there, and the blazing orange sunsets made Tsang the most inviting place in the world. No wonder the westerners coveted this land and made it their first military settlement.

The beautiful forest of Tsang that lined the landscape reminded Ben of Sekou his dad had so much talked about. There was a low-lying area where runoff from high ground collected after rain. Sometimes dense stands of acacia woodland would grow there where water was the easiest to find, unlike in the desert.

Swallowed up by the jungle, thickly scented spruce branches clutched at his clothes, slapped against his chest and shredded his hands when Ben led the visit to his newly acquired land. Sekou was impressed and proud of his son.

Cottonwoods had complemented this thick forest that carpeted the uplands along its length and young trees little more than twice a man's height had sprung up where thick grass carpeted the narrow strip.

After acquiring this vast domain in Tsang, Ben settled in quickly with a clear goal; to become the most successful person he had ever known. He planted all sorts of exotic fruits and comestible plants on his farm and was still teaching. In the meantime, he was still accepting all means of payments. He went to great cities and bought what was needed in the village and sold the items for a profit. He also reared all sorts of animals and became a distributor of choice for foreigners and big retailers in the large nearby cities.

He was not afraid of either failure or success. He perceived that people who are afraid of success or failure do not even bother attempting anything great. Such people lack belief in their abilities and their potential. They think that they will be judged and mock by people if they fail. So, they do not try anything meaningful. Such people also see success and source of envy. Conversely, Ben was rather convinced that he could achieve anything he set his mind to do. This was the main reason why he left Sekou.

He had an extreme sense of belief in himself and his abilities. Beside his self-confidence, Ben had mastered the goal-setting process. Right from his departure from Sekou he had a plan, despite having nothing. He had a set of short-term, mid-term and long-term goals. For example, his short-term goal was to find shelter and accept any menial job, so he could survive and enrol in his courses. His mid-term goals were to start his own business, and though he had no capital he worked as a teacher and tutored students after school to make extra money.

To attract different types of customers, Ben accepted payment in goods, money, and other things in exchange for his services. This quickly gave him the assets he needed to buy his farm and grow his livestock. He then invested in education. He also built a school as he became a landowner while continuing to diversify his income. Most of all, he was unsatisfied with what he had and where he was in life. This quest for improvement helped Ben to explore everything that was available and the greater things he could achieve.

He became the owner of the first modern private school in the area. His aim was to train resilient and successful pupils with a 'can do' mentality. Soon, people were coming from other parts of the country to study at his school.

When the Germans landed in Tsang, his reputation had grown beyond the reputation of the two native kings of Leke and Foto, and he was approached for all the critical decisions and strategic meeting in the county. He was made the King of Tsang although he did not ask for such honours. Before its acquisition by Ben, Tsang remained uninhabited because the two kings were fighting over this piece of land and when Ben acquired it, he kept the name Tsang and the Germans, unable to pronounce, the word renamed the place Dschang, which remains the name used until today. Everyone knows the city of Dschang nowadays, thank to Ben.

Chapter 5

Reach Your Goal; You're Invictus

A dream will remain a dream until it is realised. Although all dreams can be achieved, not every dream is achieved as most dreams stay in their bearer's mind and with their bearers until they pass away or transit to either paradise or hell. As such, heaven and hell are full of the unachieved dreams of billions of spiritual beings who have visited this planet earth. Each person came here with a purpose, but the majority returned, not only with their unfulfilled dreams, but sadly without even discovering the reason for which they came into this world.

Human beings fail their society just by failing to achieve their purpose and dreams. Those who reach their true purpose improve everyone's life. The scarcity and lack are created by those who do not live up to their calling and duties.

In his short life, Ben had seen too many people who had been unable to realise their potential. He knew hundreds of people from Mengang who passed away, leaving nothing to be remembered for. These people were quickly forgotten because they made no difference in anyone's life. They met their land in a derelict state and left it no better off. Only a few people like Sekou have transformed lives through personal efforts and will. Sekou, Ben's dad, by chance or fortune had managed to make a difference. His experience was worth replicating, given the number of human beings who had benefited from it.

Whether at Mengang, Leke, Africa or throughout the world, billions of people are just living without a sense of purpose. They dram and kill their own dreams and prefer to struggle throughout their existence on earth. It is as if their found purpose was to struggle- instead of achieving and impacting the world. They lived a life of suffering, hunger and lack, not because the world lacks anything; anyone can succeed, and no one can become successful by preventing anyone else by doing so. Just as birds don't collide in the sky, so can men thrive on earth, sharing the same space if they want, existing resources and discovering new ones.

Anyone can seek opportunities. However, to find them, one needs to know what they are looking for. Do the billions of people who are struggling across the globe know what they are looking for? They certainly don't and if they don't know what they are looking for, it is not surprising that they are unable to recognise something of value when they see it? Certainly not. So, no failure is down to bad luck. **Failure is when the wrong application of knowledge collides with action.**

Ben made a conscious decision to succeed in his right. Long ago, on that market day, years before they were expelled from Mengang, his discovery led to an eye-opening revelation: That he could achieve something he had never seen or heard of. Perhaps what he wanted to achieve existed, but living in an empty village like Mengang, his inspiration could only have come from a divine source and by insightful revelation. His dream was to make an impact on the world. This is probably what many people do not understand. Most people are preoccupied about meeting their daily needs, despite having the ability to feed the world. They stop at Midway instead of going all the way to the land of more than enough.

As for the source of all successes, God, the creator is committed to each human being's success. When you succeed, he is the first to be happy; he prides himself on seeing his creatures achieving their full potential. When you succeed, he gets the glory out of your success. It does not matter whether you say thank you to God or not. You should be thankful; but whether are you thankful or not, he is still glorified. Imagine building a car that becomes the best car in the world. The car may not thank you or acknowledge you for creating it, but people will surely admire his maker, and possibly know him without any advertisement.

When you invent a car, the car may not even think that you created it; it may not have that consciousness to understand its origin. However, despite this ingratitude, you remain the creator or the inventor of the car, and will still be proud of your invention, regardless.

A mechanic has a purpose of mending cars, a teacher has an assignment to teach children, a barman's role is to sell drinks. A farmer's role is to grow crops and feed people. So, when they succeed in what they do, they are happy. People who have benefited from their efforts may not thank them, but this does not prevent them from taking credit from being good at what they do. When people's celebration of your car makes you happy, you are by this simple act glorified. When people appreciate the produce of your farm, they may not expressly say it to you. They may not even know your name, but the appreciation of work of your hands speaks for your efforts.

Hence, people's celebration of their successes glorifies God, even if they do not expressly thank him for creating and helping them to succeed. In fact, God is happy because your success is the reason, he created you! When you achieve your purpose, God cannot be unhappy. Through your achievement, God identifies himself as exceedingly great and is satisfied with himself.

We are born of God, and those that believe in Jesus Christ are the sons of God, says the Bible. Each human, therefore, has God's attributes, though they may not have God's substance, they nonetheless have a mandate to do great things. If you give up, you have left the world without answers to your allocated lots of problems to solve. You are a problem solver in your own right. Failure to do your part is missing the mark, in other words, sinning. You now understand: Get up and walk to your assignment! There is a reward for having confidence in your abilities. If you throw your confidence away, you lose the reward. If you do not understand the value of confidence, you will miss your assignment, hence, your reward.

Anything you want to do on earth can be done because you have a divine mandate and authority on earth to do anything imaginable. Didn't he say that all things are possible for those who believe? The world is not only for the gifted, because everyone is gifted. The world is for the intrepid, the courageous and the brave who act. Those who are not scared to dare. The ones who just go for what they want and believe that they are owners and masters of their achievements.

The West, in general, is always a step forward because they believe in their assignment and their power to make things happen. They use their minds to bring the products of their imagination to fore. At times, they believe that they can be as good as God, and they are confident of having God's attributes. This self-confidence is at the centre of all progress made in developed countries. Conversely, Africans do not believe in their "deity" and their unlimited power and ability to subdue the earth. They do not value and understand who they are. Those who think that they are made for success always succeed.

Those who believe they are poor, remain poor. Most systems and intimidation put in place so far by some developed powers are made to elude Africans of their self-confidence, to ensure that they lose a sense of self-belief and see themselves as inferior, unable do anything without others. This creates a community of dependent people and followers.

Unconsciously, Africans have pledged allegiance to such powers. They have become "blessed, yes yes". With their alliances, they unwittingly give up their rights and resources, their system and values to follow others. Their lack of confidence reduces them to followers.

Your illimitationism is squashed with a psychological damnation if you keep following other peoples' agendas. No mentally able man should fail. No mentally stable man should live other people's dreams. No mentally healthy individual can miss their way.

The secret is never to give up until you find the right path to your destination. Your destiny, your hike should be aimed at the right to reach and to establish dominion there. Nobody can take away your confidence without your permission. **You permit others to rule you, either through fear or capitulation.** Without a doubt, each of us can do great things, but to do so, our thoughts must be great. **Great thoughts generate great actions.**

Those who think big accomplish big things. The question is, why doesn't everyone think big? Because humans are unconsciously a product of their environment, and the environment has a huge impact on our thinking. The thoughts that determine our conditions are those we entertain, accept, or tolerate.

Ben only allowed positive thoughts and had control over his actions. His actions, his tongue, his higher self, pure and right, reflected the quality of his spirit being. He was led by the pure spirit which indwelled him. During their adventure in the forest, only positive thoughts and a strong will power kept them going. Despite their situation, they had health, happiness, joy, love, kindness, patience, and a higher drive for achievement. Only this mindset can push one to achieve great projects.

Ben was determined to build skyscrapers, suspension bridges, churches, mansions, and universities.

It is true that human beings are masters in copying what happens in their immediate environment, but most of the time, they quickly choose options that are less sacrificial. Options that require fewer efforts, whether for good or bad results. Only a few people choose behavioural patterns that require hard work, abnegation, and self-sacrifice. Such people are those who know exactly what they want in life. The rest are just followers, who copy the actions of their neighbours, and by so doing create a culture where things are done in that way. Bad or good. This is how national and cultural traits are formed. By doing things in the same way, people become attracted to those who will mimic their behavioural patterns. This creates affinities and affiliations. Lazy people quickly find other lazy people to mingle with, no matter where they find themselves. Contrariwise, if they were to find themselves surrounded by hardworking people without any possibility of running away, they will at first experience a dramatic shift. However, they will subsequently start the process of preadaptation, re-adaptation, and dedication.

Poor people tend to gravitate to poor people, and rich people attract wealthy people. Thieves walk with thieves, and so on. But if by nature you are rich and decide to follow poor people, you will become annihilated and lost. You will start mimicking poor people or following their agenda instead of being and remaining yourself. By so doing, you will be lost in a stranger's land, living per someone else's identity.

Poverty has never been ordained, neither by nature nor God. Nature is incredibly rich, and God is unlimited. All there is, seen or unseen, imagined or not yet, already is in God. **Man chooses to live in poverty in exchange for an easy ride,**

as opposed to giving what it takes to get what he is destined for.

Living in poverty is giving up the race in exchange for a little now, irrespective of the consequences. No one will ever reach their purpose without postponing the current gratification for the ultimate prize. Reaching your purpose may require more readiness, more serving, more training, more studying, more sacrifice and giving up the ease of now to achieve something greater.

Poverty is an unwise choice for an unwise man. **It is the end destination for a fool and a state of mind of a lost sheep**. It is a choice; those who end up in it, have done so by volition, by wilfully neglecting their responsibilities for self and humans. No one can gain alone from their success, and poor people are those whose have nothing to bring to the human species. They wander in search of small chunks for the next pressing needs. Their lives and ambitions are built around eating and mating. Consequently, they end up with less or nothing. The Bible says that "those who have more are given more and those who have little, the little they have is taken away from them".

Poor people are those who are only concerned with the here and now. By the time they sort out their present needs, the next need is already calling them. They are trapped forever in this struggle to meet only their current needs. This is what most people in the world spend their time doing. Their short-sightedness causes them to miss the path to permanent victory and freedom. Therefore, they will never stop complaining or shifting the blame for their situation onto something else.

Poor people do not know they are the cause of their demise, and this explains why any assistance can only temporarily alleviate their condition. If they want a permanent solution to their situation, they must find it themselves. This solution is never far away from their reach. There is a problem to solve everywhere life is possible, and freedom from lack comes from problem-solving. Those who are courageous enough to suspend their current focus on the now, to give attention to the steps to take ahead, end up finding the right path to success.

Poverty, like success, is indiscriminate. If you follow the laws of success, the doors of success will open to you. So, it is with poverty, and your exit point is your choice. Success or poverty are neutral, they are never over interested in you nor under disinterested in you. They respond to your call, to the level of your commitment with either of them. Those who remain in poverty have pledged allegiance to poverty, and those who stay rich have signed a long-term contract with prosperity. If you break the rules, there will be a penalty.

Success can meet us everywhere. Everyone is here to achieve their ultimate goal and purpose; firstly, for themselves and secondly for the benefit of the whole human race. If you fail to achieve your purpose, you become a liability to others. This is the origin of greed and wars. People are made to influence each other, for a mutually beneficial process. By using each other's strengths each benefit, but failure to do so results in a lost. When one cannot bring anything to the table, he may receive for a while, but the supply will eventually stop when others realise that they cannot keep giving without any output.

The supply stops naturally, as the poor man is not offering anything of value. Whatever had no added value is devalued and abandoned or assessed as useless. In some cases, we can say that a poor man is useless to himself and others, in the sense that he is not bringing in anything of value to either himself or others. If he were, they would be willing to pay the price for his services, thus giving him the means to earn a decent living.

Poor people rely on others and use what would have rightfully belonged to others for their survival and preservation, thereby creating a shortage where there should have been abundance. Lack of output generates scarcity; greed and conflict are the implications of a lack of output of many- those who are so called poor. To some extent, poor people are robbers and cheaters. They believe they have the same rights as everyone else. They do not know in fact that they are the cause of lack. Had they contributed their part to society, everyone would have been better off. This is the reason why they cheat and rob others without knowing. They are unconscious and ignorant people. In fact, if they were not ignorant, they would not have been lost in the first place.

Everyone should be mindful of their behaviour. Each should thrive to achieve their purpose and earthly goals. This cannot be done by following the crowd. It is a personal affair and requires a sharp mind, deep thinking, and relentlessness. If you want to avoid poverty, you need to find your purpose and pursue it. You can do it without fail because you can do so. You are Invictus.

Chapter 6

Living in a Treasure Land, But Dying of Hunger

From Tchouale, you continue to Kemtsop and from there, you proceed uphill to Ziden Foto which is a small settlement of about 100 souls. After Ziden Foto, continuing on the main road, you linger downhill and cross the river that marks the border between Leke and Fotetsa and head uphill again to the crossroad of Fotetsa. From the crossroad, just at the outskirts of Fotetsa centre, you advance downhill and pass the King's Palace, then down again and slightly uphill, passing below Fotetsa primary school. The main school is on the hill and the main road under.

Following this path, you cross Lefock the river and continuing up the hill again you are at Makong. From Makong, you go down and up to the plateau leading to the white house of Pele. You are in New Mengang. From Pele's White House, head down again to Nzinbing. This Nzinbing is different from the Forest now known as Sekou. About 5.5 miles from Tsang or Dschang City you reach a beautiful spot called Nzinbing, situated between Lewetschou and Tsenlah, located on the outskirts of Fotetsa. From Nzinbing, you could see Tsang, Letieu and Saa'Nzock, which happened to be Ben's ancestral land. Mountains surrounded the area all the way to Watseng and Goudeng, and further up there is a series of hills that never end until Mock and Coupé.

This beautiful village of Fotetsa was a home to all kinds of birds, animals, trees, and streams. The soil was rich and wasted no time in producing any types of crops planted. It was dense with vegetation. The surrounding mountains made the place look like a crossroad to heaven. In the more fecund areas of this beautiful land, centuries-old trees with sprawling limbs guarded the darkness, blotting out any sunlight. This is what the locals dreaded and named it the dark forest of the gods. Passers-by threw items into the forest as a sacrifice in exchange for blessings from the gods of the forest. At the entrance of the forest, a small house was built and was regularly swept by Petro, the guardian of the gods. Whoever wanted a special blessing had to bring Petro oil and livestock. Depending on the seriousness of their case, one could be asked to offer a sacrifice; anything from a chicken to a cow. Petro would use goats, hens or roosters for the ceremonies. In reality, he ate or sold them!

The forest was mind-blowing, with all sorts of exotic trees and plants. Perhaps this is what made the villagers call it the forest of gods. The bark of some of the trees was mottled and splotched as if soup had been frozen in time on its surface. Clumpy combs of wet moss dangled from their rotten boughs. Underneath the moss, lethal larkspur peppered the mulchy floor. A pungent tang oozed from every sentient being in the forest. Bewailing sounds ghosted through the three day and night. Whether it was from victim or victor only the forest could tell, as few people, like in Mengang, dared to enter its depths.

It was truly a place to make your veins freeze over. However, for lovers of nature, it was a paradise on earth. At nightfall, the moonlight would fade, creating new shadows and dark patches around the surrounding mountains. The wind wailed between the distorted trunks, carrying the sickly stink of dry rot. A path surrounded by high trees wound through the middle of the forest. It was like a corridor. Lifting your face in its midst, you could see both the light and shadow dance across your skin. Bees hummed in and out of the pennyroyal, signs that flowers abounded in the area. By day or night, you could inhale a dry rot smell all around.

The trees stood utterly still like statues in a museum and no leaf dared to fall when the wind was not blowing, however, all changed so quickly when it blew. For example, branches creaked at the command of the wind or beneath the footsteps of passers-by. At times, it was a Jumble with squirrels that were chattering, leaves that were rustling, wind whistling around trunks, disturbing the leaves. Here and there, you could hear birds singing, insects humming or chirping and animals rooting in the underbrush rustling. Lizards scrabbled on tree bark and the limbs crashed to the ground.

Crackling underfoot were breaking branches when someone walked by and clattering leaves. The sighing wind or groaning trees, squawking birds or hostile screeches from animals was frightening, as panting and barking yips or ruffling and ticking sounds continued.

Here and there you could hear tapping and rattling noises, some animals grating the beat of paws against a path with harmonic rhythm, and you could see green, brown, dead fallen trees, logs, branches, twigs, fallen leaves, ferns, underbrush, moss, brambles, thickets, ivy, berry bushes, pine needles, pine cones, acorns, insects, rabbits, birds, lizards, mice, foxes, spider webs, deer, sun-dappled, shady shafts of light, branches blowing, deer paths, dark, thick, thin, sparse, colourful rose hips, flowers, bird nests, shifting patterns of light, cold trunks covered with moss, bugs, stillness, beetles, grass hassock, caves, rocky, moist ravines, creeks, streams, willows, oak trees, sap crusts, aspen, spruce boughs, seed pods, decay, wild mushrooms, toadstools.

The forest offered an unending catalogue of magnificent sceneries. You could paint and paint again but would soon be out of descriptive words to name all that you could see or hear around. It was a unique environment that perhaps could only be seen in this part of the world; its inhabitants were unable to recognise the paradise they had at hand.

When passing through this village one day, Ben was thrilled by the beauty and potential of the land. As a first sight, he fell in love with the place. He wanted this land at all costs. He could transform it into a human-made island, a thriving city. A land of opportunities. It was also a perfect spot where Ben could build his castle. This location was the steep slopes of Nzinbing, on the hilltops of this enchanting place.

Abundant with freshwater springs, Fotetsa was far away from the sea. This beautiful mosaic of mountains and forest was a perfect spot for someone who was in search of silence and tranquillity.

The inhabitants of this beautiful village only lived in a small agglomeration, side by side, in the vicinity of the village and close to the main road leading to Dschang with the rest of the land quasi-unbridled, wild, and neglected. This made it even easier for Ben to acquire the land, because the villagers did not see any value in it, and did not care what happened to it. They cursed God every day for making them descendants of such an ugly and remote place. They wished they were born closer to the cities. For them, they were lost in the forest in the middle of nowhere, and their primary concern was to meet their daily demand for food. The forest, mountains and streams only served the purpose of producing the fruits that they gathered each day and the animals that they hunted.

No one thought that something good could be done with this apparently lost land. Likewise, no one imagined that better living conditions were possible in Fotetsa. No one had ever seen its potential, except for Ben. People spent their time lamenting about their conditions and no villager thought about growing crops other than what was necessary for personal consumption. No wonder why they went hungry every day, particularly when the hunting or gathering was not fruitful. Despite streams abounding, no one thought of using them for irrigation. Villagers all depended on the mercy of the rain for farming activities.

Why was this village's potential hidden from its inhabitants for so long? Ben pondered. To him, it was a forgotten paradise. As you strolled the village's narrow streets, it was evident that people

POOR LAND OR POOR MINDS

took life very easy or rather, not so seriously. Was it due a lack of ambition, imagination, or foresight? It was hard to tell. Nevertheless, their inability to ask more than what their tummy fixed as their daily penalty was evident. Even so, they often failed to have a full belly. This price was set every day and they anticipated no demand for the next day. For example, when the hunting was abundant or when they gathered more fruits than they needed for the day, they threw the rest away, and when, the next day the hunting was unfruitful, they regretted their previous actions. However, they never learned from their mistakes.

They saw no further than the end of their noses; everything they hunted or gathered each day had to be finished on the same day. This was their daily lot as they lived a life of struggle; they were waiting for the day they would leave this temple to meet their ancestors in the heavens or hells.

Most people in this village believed in life after death. But, central to their belief system was that their mortal ancestors created the heavens and earth and that life on earth was a punishment rather than a blessing. This was the reason they accepted their conditions and believed fervently that they had no power to change it. Their hope was for a better life after death. They even went as far as believing that their dead ancestors were wiser the living. The question is, if they had not done anything better while living on earth, how could they suddenly become the wisest after death? It was difficult to convince the poor of this village that they could change their fate. They firmly believed their fate was sealed by God, who completed the punishment by condemning them to a desolate land. This mindset kept them in a permanent state of deprivation, ill health, desolation, and poverty.

From time to time, to appease God, they offered sacrifices, including giving the forest something from their daily finds.

The good thing about the people of Fotetsa was their ability to live in harmony with their environment. Although they rendered no justice to animals, by making them pay the price for their own lives for daring to venture into their forests, they preserved nature and surely applied the concept of sustainable development.

The land Ben purchased had never been exploited and none one had ever lived there. The main agglomeration was at the outskirts of Nzinbing.

Populated with only 11 families, Nzinbing, within Fotetsa, was a tiny, autonomous community. Even today, it is still possible to distinguish the inhabitants of this village from those of a neighbouring community by their pronunciation, accent, and facial features. They built their houses with mud, except those who had made their fortune in the city, and who, for the respect of their culture and traditions, returned to build better houses with cement. There were only three of these well-built houses in Fotetsa. The close contact between the inhabitants of Fotetsa and people of Dschang influenced the architecture of the village.

Ben discovered this paradise when one of his beloved employees, who happened to be from this village, died and he attended the funerals. This is how he discovered this village and fell in love with its beauty. He then decided to purchase hectares of land, as usual for personal use. He acquired two-thirds of the land in the area and decided not only to transform the land but also to build his castle there.

In this part of the village, just behind the agglomerations, by the roadside, there was an abundance of timber, mango trees, guavas, papaya, prunes; all kinds of fruits and vegetables that rendered the village virtually self-sufficient in essential goods. But, as already mentioned, no effort from any villager was made above the required limits of their daily needs to get more from the land. They did not know that their village had treasures of immense importance, and that special care was needed to unleash its full potential and to protect them.

Beauty is in the eye of the beholder, they say. How many people, like the Fotetsa, live in a gold mine that they ignore? How are many people, like these people, live in total poverty despite having enormous wealth around them? Why don't they see it? What prevents them from noticing it? Is it probably their lack of imagination or their inability to think and to see beyond the surface? Everyone possesses potential, and the ability to think and see beyond the five senses, but it is impossible to perceive beyond their immediate environment without the help of deep thoughts. Shall we then conclude that poor people fail to use this ability? The answer is simply yes! The hidden treasures of this world can only be discovered if one first uses his mind and use it well. For example, going to the moon was first a concept in the mind. Before man invented tools to locate it and to go there.

You must use the power of your imagination to see beyond the physical. It is the same for new discoveries and inventions; people need to use their imagination and thoughts to discover ideas and concepts.

Perhaps the people of Fotetsa needed to be alerted or informed that everything exists for a purpose. Despite being a dreamland for someone, Fotetsa was just an ordinary place for its natives. They did not value their land, while Ben saw its potential at first sight. Perhaps this is proper to all Africans who sit on gold mines but see it as useless. When Ben put in an offer to buy the land, no villager dared turn it away. He acquired it and decided to build his residence. He called it the Castle of Fotetsa, or TCF.

Ben is one of the rarest Africans who understand the power of his mind. He is one of the few in the world who understand that the Spirit controls the world. That each invention, each realisation, each achievement starts from the mind.

Africa has all resources the world craves for, but Africans are unable to explore and exploit them. But they decide to exploit it, they dig it with their hands with little result instead of inventing the right explore and to exploit them on a larger scale. This behaviour is widespread across the continent. It seems as if African people do not make a conscious effort to discover the hidden treasures of their land. Consequently, they always depend on others to tell them of such treasures, including what could be done with them. Isn't it curious?

The people of Fotetsa used their sight instead of their mind to guide them through life. They depended on what was served on a plate; what they could see with their eyes ready for immediate use for their physical and physiological satisfaction.

They totally ignored the importance of processing, investigating and transformation. This resignation was the main cause of their poor social conditions. Their lack of knowledge, attention and contemplation and application knowledge was the root of their poverty. Their poverty was not caused by any circumstance's exterior to themselves. The cause of their deprivation was internal and self-created and inflicted. They had, by their own will, given up their treasures to others in exchange for peanuts. Fotetsa mimicked typical African widespread behaviour.

To do great things and to see beyond the surface, people need to use their mind. Images that are formed in the mind can inspire creativity. So, creativity starts with imagination which is a function of the mind. To achieve great things, Africans need to condition their subconscious to see above their self-limiting and obliterating ignorance. To discover their inner strengths, they need to sever their overdependence on others and make a conscious effort to see with their own eyes, the treasures that abounds in their land. What attracts people to their lands can also attract their curiosity. What attracts people to their land can inspire them and fuel their creativity, provided they are willing to use an investigative and explorative process- looking with their inner eyes instead of using their six senses. They need to make use of their mind!

People from Fotetsa devalued their precious possessions and wasted no time in giving up their land in exchange for temporal gratification. This lack of foresight always leads to post-sales regrets. Haven't we heard Africans crying that their natural resources were sold for peanut? But have they stop falling in the same trap? The answer is no! they don't learn from their mistake.

Fotetsa was like a miniature fortress. Local tradition abounded with tales to make one dream of a world where manna will fall from heaven. None of these tales invited people to use the power of their inner thoughts to improve their living conditions. None of the tales invited people to imagine that they had the power to make of their better. None of these tales stopped them from selling almost their entire village to a total stranger.

None of the stories stirred people up to go beyond the ordinary. None of the tales pushed people to see themselves as worthy and able to transform their environment for the better. All the tales instead invited submission and resignation; it painted humans as either waiting for divine intervention or to see their limitations. No wonder they possessed such a limited worldview.

None of these villagers dared to question why the Europeans were so eager to get their hands on the land around the city, nor did they question why Ben was so interested in this land. They focused only on the money they could make from the proceeds of the land and therefore relinquishing their land to Ben was not a difficult task for them. By selling their land, they thought that the proceeds would help them to escape poverty. It certainly gave them a reprieve for few months, but after the money had finished, they returned to the same conditions as before. None of them used their money to invest in their future. They spent it on food. The village was now 90% owned by Ben who saw great potential in what people took for granted.

Like people of Fotetsa, all Africans see nothing extraordinary about their land, their gifts and talents or their potential. Almost of African's precious resources and treasures have been discovered by non-Africans. The reason is simple: Africans don't want to waste their time investigating. They do not want to spend their time finding solutions. They want to be solutions users rather than solution finders, ignoring that each human is supposed to be a solution bringer; a problem solver to someone or to the world. Each person's earning is based on the importance of the problem they solve. For example, a baker solves' someone needs for bread and a buyer solves the baker's monetary problem and with the proceeds of its sales, the baker solves a car dealer's problem, etc. If you solve no problem, you will have nothing or no income to solve your own problem. If you cannot solve someone's problem, no one can solve yours.

To be free from lack, one should focus on bringing solutions to other people's problems. If you have nothing to offer others, it's hard to receive from anyone, unless it is through someone's act of kindness or charity. If you cannot be useful to others, it might be difficult for you to be free from needs because no one will need you. A House owner will need a builder and a hungry person will need the farmer's produce and so goes the world. Your offering attracts income that helps you to meet your own needs, I insist! Whether in Fotetsa, Leke or Melong, most Africans people behave in the same way, live in the same way, and suffer from similar types of issues: hunger, poverty, and low self-esteem. They do not recognise that their key priority should be on altering the way they think rather than focusing on survival. They ignore that a lasting solution should come from their ability to think and their ability to cater for other people's needs or for solving the world's problems, rather than grasping whatever they have to meet their present needs. Everyone one who uses without replenishing will eventually run out of supply.

It is amazing how, despite its richness, the land that was sold to Ben was neglected and no one thought that its streams could be used for irrigation to produce more crops at any time of the year. No one from the village saw that polished furniture or better shelters could be made from its trees. Ben was laughed and mocked at when he acquired the land. People thought he was a fool. However, for him, it was a delight and an excellent opportunity to achieve his dream.

He saw in the land, an ideal spot to build his castle. In honour of the great land he built "The Castle of Fotetsa" TCF. The great castle, the only one n the county.

He planned on transforming the land and marvelling people around the world. Visitors would come from all parts of the globe to visit his castle. He would then cash in through tourism and build hotels and skyscrapers, just as he imagined when he was little. He would start with helicopters for people to see the beauty of the mountains and the forest from above.

Ben was closer to his dream. Fewer people would have imagined this possible. In less than 25 years after his A levels, Ben had become very wealthy. He owned colleges, lands, ships, and cars.

He started chasing his dream aged 30 with no qualification, and now in his mid-fifties, he was getting closer to his goals. In fact, he now had everything he had ever wanted from life; nonetheless, he still had new projects and new dreams. He had not put his mind to rest and his thoughts were still thriving for new solutions to human problems. The world was still in need of better things.

Ben's quest to find solutions to human problems was the secret behind his success. His ability to think creatively brought him success, and his self-confidence was the driving force for his achievements. His mindset was critical in creating his present conditions. His wealth was the product of his thought processes.

Ben's situation suggests that a person is what he thinks, feels, and believes. **A person's outward manifestation is the result of his deepest thoughts. Through unconscious impartment of his mind, a man determines his future and his living conditions.** Through his thought process, he determines his future. A man presses upon his environment to transform his whole experience, whether real or physical, by his way of thinking. **A mindset prone and addicted to improvement will make improvements. A mindset allergic to poverty will repel poverty by finding alternative solutions to fight poverty.**

Ben was convinced that millions of people could change their conditions and position through their ability to think differently. According to Emerson, "A man is what he thinks all day long." The people of Tsang, Fotetsa, Letieu and Mengang were poor, not because their land was meagre, but because they believed their inability to overcome poverty. Their thought process created their living conditions. Their state of mind created their state of being. What they thought all day long created the conditions they lived every day. They believed that their land, with all its richness, could not deliver them from their conditions. They thought that working for someone else was the best alternative, or that by a divine accident, a man would fall from the heavens to transform their way of life. Their belief was, in fact, the cause of their stagnation and downfall. Their belief was dictating their living conditions. So, it goes!

All over the world, people are bound by their beliefs. **A conviction of freedom frees, and a feeling of poverty impoverishes. A conviction of glory brings glory, and a belief of scarcity brings poverty. A belief in good health brings good health, and a belief in impossibilities hinders progress**.

Miracles happen all over the world, yet, miracles are only called miracles to those who ignore the power of their thoughts and their spiritual dimension. Those who know successful people's behaviour will not be surprised to see them at the top of their glory because they are aware of the think and act.

In addition to self-belief, people are bound by the beliefs, opinions, training, and environmental influences that they let sink into their subconscious.

The desire for true peace of mind, abundance, and security are real and inherent to all men but few experience these things because if their self-limiting thoughts. One can only achieve what he thinks is possible. The Fotetsa had a poverty-type mindset, and they lived in poverty-stricken conditions.

Ben was a man with a mind filled with ideas of wealth, and he kept attracting everything he needed. He dreamed of building his castle in a spot like Fotetsa, without even knowing that such a spot existed. One day by pure coincidence, he found himself there. Had he not foreknown what he was looking for, he would not have discovered the land or acquire it. The discovery of the land was the opportunity he was looking for. **A man is never stranger to his opportunities. He knows in advance what will be an opportunity and what will not. Those who see possibilities in everything lack focus. Those who have no opportunities lack foresight.**

Had Ben arrived at Fotetsa 20 years earlier, he would not have had the same reaction, possibly, he wouldn't have acquired the land.

In fact, he would not have had money, or the courage to purchase the land. Opportunities occur when preparedness is met with circumstances, and opportunities are secured by action. If you don't know what you are looking for, you will find nothing, even if you suddenly find yourself in a gold mine. Present £1,000,000 and a banana to a child who is hungry, he will choose the banana even though he could buy acres of banana farms with the £1,000,000. Equally, if you offer a choice between food worth £1000 and an opportunity worth billions of pounds to an African, they will choose food. Because in the food they see their immediate needs being met, whereas they may not identify the wealth hidden in the opportunity. They are looking for food and not something beyond the present moment. They are not thinking about what they could do with good ideas; they are interested in how they can survive today and what they can make out of your present offering. Have we not heard many Africans say that they were more interested in what you have to offer them than your ideas? They usually say, "I don't need your ideas, do I eat your ideas?" As such, they are not acting better than a child, and this is one of the main reasons behind Africa's problems.

This is also the reason why the Fotetsa could not see beyond a chain of mountains and forests that surrounded their villages. They saw no good in it because they didn't know what they wanted apart from satisfying their need for food. They cared less about what could become of their land even though their only possession they had was their land.

With that land, Ben redesigned that whole village. Out of the mess, a city was being built. Out of the chaos, an order was being restored through one man's thoughts.

A transformation of a place begins with an idea. Ben thought of linking together the many streams around the village, just below the mountains to create an island. The continued flow of water could be used for navigation and people could go around the village through the waterway. In areas where there were hills, they dug a tunnel underneath to create a way.

After started the project of building his castle, people arrived from everywhere to look for work in Fotetsa. Everyone was talking about the wonders of its transformation. Young people from the village, who had left their village a long time before in search of work in the cities were returning to work in their village. Concomitantly with the building of his island, Ben started building his castle in addition to the shops and hotels in the village. He linked all parts of the village with a road and improved the roads leading to the city of Dschang.

He used the lakes in the community to grow fish. This was the beginning of aquaculture, which had never been experimented with in this part of the world. He also created a zoo.

He imported species of animals that could not be found in the village. He built schools, hospitals and brought in electricity from the city. The village was booming; people from faraway lands started pouring into the village. This formerly mistreated and forgotten land was becoming a jewel as its transformation was taking shape. No villager could believe what he was seeing.

Soon, the castle was built, the tower was built, the shopping mall was built, the church was built, the village hall was built, better roads were built, and the canal was completed. The village became an island; boats filled the rivers that ringed the whole village. It was possible to go by boat all the way to Worri through NKam.

The government sent someone to represent the central government in the village and made this tiny village a subdivision of Dschang. All these changes were down to one man's ability to imagine something extraordinary. He believed nothing was impossible. The transformation didn't come from a mere observation of the physical appearance of the village, but through the power of an imaginative mind. The power of thoughts once again had spoken.

This goes to show that great cities, great countries, great businesses are people's brainchildren. First, they are the product of imagination; they are then brought to life by will and determination. So why do millions of people lack access to water in Africa, a land 90% served by water? Why are people dying of hunger in Africa, a land full of riches and endowed with natural fertilisers? Something has gone wrong, not in the land but its population's minds.

African people have lost their minds, and thereby, lost their respect and grip in their own lives. What is naturally, fundamentally, and essentially theirs has been rejected, neglected, and sold at a vile price, because of their short sight and lack of imagination and willingness to think. They have surrendered their right to succeed. Each of these poor people is a wealthy man and woman, essentially and potentially, but their lack of will to seek, to do and to be who they should be has led them to worldly losses. They are living in hell here on earth. This should not have been the case. Everyone is made for success; everyone is made to perfection and satisfaction. Each person has the right to be here and to live a happy life. This can only start in the mind, our only link to the eternal God. Only through the proper use of our mind can we tap into the truth, the source of freedom and wealth.

Limit not your mind and your life will be unlimited. Limit not your will, and your quest for greater things will be achieved. Limit not your strengths and efforts, and your dream will be achieved. Go for it as if nothing else matters, and you will see and touch the results. Fear not, for if you fail, it will only be for a moment, but mostly it will serve as a learning curve. Fear not, for they will yell and curse at your failure, however, their opinions about you will change nothing of your true nature and substance. Those laughing at you now will claim to be your friends when you have reached your destiny and shone like a diamond. They will want to justify their actions at that time, but will it matter? No, because their mockeries and stupidities have made you stronger. Their yelling, in fact, pushed you to extract the best from yourself.

You would be a miracle, a unique person, like God and a God of your own, from your own choice, if you chose to. You do not create yourself, but you create your circumstances. You do not determine where you are born, but you can choose where you live. You can determine what you do with the gift of life.

Ben hoped that his achievements would encourage others. To create a momentum in the community, he decided to organise a party after the construction of his castle. People who knew Ben from childhood would be at the party including the King of Mengang, who plotted to expel his family from the village. This was not revenge. It was a lesson: he who is willing can become great, will become great if he wants. Will people learn the lesson in other parts of the country or in the continent? When Ben's palace was completed, he invited his family and friends to the grand opening of the Castle of Fotetsa, Ben's residence, in the very spot he chose, and his castle built just as he wanted.

Chapter 7

The Castle of Fotetsa

Ben smiled and glanced across the vast room where his portraits hung on the wall. He was already in his late 60s. However, he still looked youthful his body bared resemblance to that of a 35-year-old. His fair complexion glowed with a hint of brown. His eyes sparkled, and his teeth were as white as they were when he was in his twenties.

Despite spending years in the forest, he always tried to look after his body, and when he became wealthy, he continued to watch what he ate. Ben's self-discipline and his strict regime were second to none. This is probably why he remained youthful with his teeth kept intact. It would have been easy to conclude that Ben had had plastic surgery if one did not know his self-discipline. He referred to his body as the dwelling place of God, and the temple of the Holy Spirit.

The opening of his castle was a significant day for him and a key milestone in his life. The grand opening of his Castle was a unique and one of the rarest achievements in Fotetsa. Ben had invited over 5000 guests and over a 1000 more attended without invites. No one was turned away as he instructed to welcome every guest, including the self-invited ones.

It was a day long ceremony and by 10 am, the castle full of guests and Ben and his immediate family were beaming with pride. Every important media of the country was there to cover the event.

When the host announced Ben's entrance, the atmosphere became light-hearted. As he entered the main hall, he came face-to-face with his guests, each incredibly excited and wanting to greet him. He gave as many hugs and handshakes as he possibly could. He looked around with a sense of pride and gratitude as he proceeded with grace and humility. Before him, at a little distance, reclined an obese old man. He had a broad, pulpy face and a stern expression. His large head was covered with grey hair, with a distinctive hat, which he wore only around his face like a frame. The hat was ancient and had lost its colours. By the look of it, you could not tell what the original colour was. The top had ceded with the weight of age and disappeared, perhaps in pieces without him noticing. His clothing, while expensive, was worn with some parts were fraying. Instantly, Ben recognised this man. He was the King of Mengang. Ben particularly invited him as a guest of honour. He remembered the importance of celebrating with his friends and foes, with his admirers and his detractors. He had decided to organise a party in front of his enemies and chartered a bus to bring people from Mengang. It seemed as if they had all forgotten about what they did to his family. It no longer mattered to Ben anyway. Every experience, whether good or bad, is a learning curve for anyone who knows where they are going. Every failure provides extra strength and assurance to those who know what they are looking for. Every recorded failure count in the process of eliminating wrong hypotheses and leads to the right solutions.

Still smiling, Ben showed his visitors his glamorous front room, which displayed the splendour of his wealth. How amazing! A man who, at 30, decided to go back to school to complete his GCSEs and who moved to Leke with nothing at all, had managed to become the richest person in his country. Everyone now knew him, including the president of his country.

Ben made his fortune in Africa without leaving his country and without receiving any help from abroad. He had only used what was already available inland. He had had found the best way to make good use of what was around him. He had used his mind to transform his life and change his position and status.

His family, which had historically only been known regionally, were now a national treasure. His father became well known throughout the country. Because of Ben, their story, including their expropriation from Mengang, had now come to light with their story being told by their aggressors themselves. These aggressors from Mengang had not changed a tiny bit. The king was the same though already very advanced in age, he was still wearing the same old ceremonial clothing he had when Ben was only a boy and shamelessly was present on this day along with his subjects.

Ben, after showing off his first front room, proceeded to one of the many living rooms. This room had large windows that showed a clear view of one of the magnificent gardens. In this artificial man-made island, everything demonstrated a typical statement of wealth, and the extent of what money could buy.

From the upper windows, you could see a clear stream that wound through the forest and underneath the hills surrounding mountains. Babbling and burbling, it sprung over the limestone rocks carefully led by inspired architecture. Pebbles whisked about in the under wash like pieces of glitter, even though the digging to accommodate small boats made it difficult to touch or feel them without an expert plunge. The water was bright and inviting.

Chords of soft light fitted by experts speared down from above, bathing its surface in gold. It was glinting with little sparkles, like a sea of diamonds blessed with an inner fire. A galaxy of dragonflies fizzed through the beams of light, wings a-glitter in the sun. It was clear that the hedgerows planted by the stream were pregnant with guava, mango, and passion fruits. The orange trees produced fruits that were comparable to none. The peaches were so juicy that only two quenched your thirst; whoever tried them was energised by their pleasant aroma. Strangely, these fruits had always been there, but the villagers of Fotetsa saw nothing unusual about them fruits. To them, all fruits of the same kind taste the same way, and all villages abounded with streams, trees, mountains and forests like theirs.

From another grand window, you could see that cockerels the size of ostriches grazed freely with some half-hidden by the carefully planted flowers, which evidenced that nothing was spared to feed them. So was it for all other species at the castle?

Still, inside the castle, the stoning scenario continued. Everything was coated with rare gold treasures, tales of derring-do and rooms seemingly touched by the endless swirl of an extraordinary and genius craft. Like the sky, this castle slowly unfolded as you walked through it; its beauty rolled out with a latent majesty designed to clobber your senses. Ordinary minds were convinced that such beauty only existed in paradise.

Ben ushered some of his visitors to a small yet splendid room. The walls were decorated with elephant Ivory and lion, panther and cobra skins completed the panacea of the ornaments.

In this part of the world, such displays were a sign of wealth beyond measure. From this room, you could see the castle's backyard facing the plains of Fotetsa from where you could see a long hedge prolonging to the horizon with a swimming pool and carefully trimmed lawn. It was evident to everyone that this lawn was designed by the finest landscape architects on the planet. The lawn and the garden of flowers had been carefully planted and maintained to the highest standard. This level of wealth was only attained by a few people on the planet. Everything was so beautiful that one would think it was the paradise. If we suppose that nothing is more beautiful than the haven, there would be no human words to qualify the real paradise if Ben had managed to accomplish such achievement on earth!

How were human beings inspired to design such a magnificent palace? Where dic their ideas originate of design, craft, colours, architecture, and landscaping came from, and how did they implement them? It was hard to convince anyone that they were not in heaven. Secretly, some people were pinching themselves to ascertain if they were still alive. All this was true and real, a proof that anything imaginable can be made through man's actions!

Ben had camels, swine, donkeys, goats, sheep, pandas, elephants, rabbits, and plenty of fish in his numerous ponds and lakes. You could also count the many varieties of birds, chickens, turkeys, ostriches, and pigeons on his farm up the hill. He had many types of animals and some of the rarest beads you could only find in few places in the world.

In the courtyard, he had over a dozen luxury cars; these did not include those in his underground car park. He also had a yacht, which he sailed on the artificial lakes and canals that he had created for his pleasure.

The palace's grand hall had a beautiful marble staircase. The grandest of all the rooms was the ballroom that served as a palace reception room for his most distinguished visitors, but it was particularly reserved for the finest moments of his life. On this day, he let people see it.

Ben's palace measured 290 metres long across the front, 250 metres deep and 42 metres high. The total floor area of the Palace, from the basement to roof, covered over 300,000 square metres, with 1,614 doors and 1040 windows. All windows were cleaned regularly, with a dedicated maintenance team on site every day to fix any damages. Over 500 people worked at his castle, earning a good salary, every single day. You can only imagine how many people came from all over the country in search of a job in Fotetsa and how many were making a living out of this formerly desolated place.

Ben's garden covered 50 acres; it had a helicopter landing area, many lakes, and a few tennis courts.

Despite his wealth, Ben had not forgotten his humble beginnings. Born into a poor immigrant family, Ben had proven to everyone that nothing was impossible for anyone who believes. He had shown that people from all walks of life could attain success and achieve their purpose in life, provided they know what they want, and are committed to making it, regardless of the setbacks. Ben had also proven that everyone's success is in his or her own hands. Most importantly, he was able to show ordinary people that wealth is not in a place but is rather a mindset, and that a well-applied mind can transform any land, anywhere in the world.

With unfailing desire to succeed, Ben transformed a whole area, and practically built a new city from scratch, implanted a monument where only 20 years earlier could never be thought possible or imaginable: The Castle of Fotetsa. The people of Fotetsa, who once believed their village was worthless, were now happily enjoying this city with zeal and pride. Most importantly, each inhabitant had started to think differently.

The village had changed forever, and almost every inhabitant had changed their profession. From fruit gatherers to hunters, villagers became entrepreneurs. Fotetsa went from an unmarked placed to a very famous place in the country. The way Ben improved and transformed the village offered a glimpse into humans' ability, potential and his unlimited power and ability to make things happen.

Chapter 8

Unaware of Our Perfection

Human beings' creative power is what makes them superior to other species. Their ability to think, to invent and to imagine helps them to do what other animals cannot do. For example, I have never seen a lion, despite its strength, improve the way it captures and eat it prays. There are no chimpanzees that have now built a house anywhere in the world, despite their intelligence. Perhaps we do not understand their world, but if they were as creative as humans, we will at least see a city built by elephants or a lion cooking it pray before eating, at least occasionally.

Creative ability rests in human's mind. Creativity helps to transform, improve, define, and determine one's environment and experience in life. One must be curious, eager, and willing to understand and to change the present state of thing or situation, before they can effectively change it. Exposed to creative people, you stand a chance of becoming creative, with a will power. Excessively exposed to poverty, you may end up agreeing with it as normal. Therefore, what one is used to, exerts a significant influence in his life, which is inevitably transformed and depends on such exposure. Therefore, to awaken our genius, we need always to contemplate great things, think high and be influenced by great ideas and acquire such habits ourselves.

Our habits are significant because they shape the course of our life. Hence, a change in habits can create a new focus and direction for our life. Change takes place in the mind. Likewise, no change can become effective without willpower and a thought process. Our consciousness of existence is a mental exercise. Therefore, to be, one must exist, and life itself cannot be lived fully without mental or spiritual wellness.

Our mental wellness determines our quality of life and our place in the world; consequently, what we can do and who we can become. A child born with mental deficiencies or incapacities is not expected to do much. It will be a miracle if he or she attempts and attains anything great. This suggests that our life depends more on the quality of our mind than the physical resources one can see in any place. With a good quality mind, it is possible to make of a place what we want. Hence, the secret of success or failure is determined by how we think- the quality of our mind.

Imagination for example is a quality of the mind and is mainly the ability to form images, situations, and things that, though may not exist in physical form, can, by this act of imagination, be created. What exists in mind already exists and can be materialised through further efforts.

For something to exist physically, it had to first exist in someone's mind first; its physical manifestation is the last stage. Some things exist and will only exist in many people' minds. In fact, if everything ever conceived in people's minds were to materialise, the world would be million times better. But only a handful of conceptions and things imagined or created in the spiritual realm are translated into material or physical forms.

Great people are those with great thoughts, and poverty or riches are the results of thought processes. Thoughts of poverty will inevitably lead to poverty and thought of abundance will lead to better conditions. Thoughts of good health will lead to good health and though of early death, will inevitably cause one to die earlier. Our consciousness is a ship, stirred and guided by our unconscious, however, our unconscious is the repository of all thoughts that dominate our psychic life.

So, when one is always thinking about poverty, they are registering it in their subconscious, which crystallises it into a physical reality and form of poverty. Because our thoughts guide and determine our life, thoughts of poverty will become our daily lot materialised by scarcity, despair, unhappiness, a lack of self-confidence and resignation. In this condition, a deprived person will continue to believe that he/she is poor and the more they believe this, the more they become poorer.

The tallest and the most handsome men do not always live a better life than others. Equally, people with the same level of education do not necessarily have the same degree of income. Furthermore, not

all those who have never been to school are poor.
If, there are rich people in very remote and poor
villages, it must imply that poverty or riches are
the results of something other than what the land
provides, or the state offers.

Since no one can share their inner mind with
another person, even though they can exchange
ideas, richness or poverty must be a result of what
goes on in everyone's mind and the way one thinks.
If human beings are born with the same facilities,
the difference will reside in the way they use their
mental faculties. Since each person is endowed
with the ability to think, and since everything that
exists is conceived in the mind, the minds that
will conceive what is most useful and innovative
will attract better endorsement, thus creating
more value that can be translated into material
accumulations of wealth.

The more creative a mind is, the more wealth
it can attract; and the more idled a mind is, the less
value they can generate and the poorer they will
be. What appears outside of us reflects what we
have within us. Solutions to human problems can
be found within, as each can tap into the infinite
spirit and limitless ability to think and imagine.

Impossibility is a self-imposed mental limitation. The only way to achieve what others may see as impossible is to believe it is possible. If my mind has no limits as to what it can think of, there is, therefore, no limits to what I can achieve. If everyone sees himself as unlimited, nothing will be impossible, and, what we do or make will no longer amount to a miracle., except if we break the law of physics.

With our mind, we have visited places without physically being there. We can revisit those places in spirit. By the same principles, we have built castles, made money, build tools that do not exist yet in a physical world. We thought of an airplane before building one. We thought of going to the moon before inventing tools to take us there. We thought of a house before building one. What we see elsewhere may inspire us to think about other things. Inspiration and imagination are a source of creativity. If you can only live by what you see or touch, you will be no different from an animal, because you will not be able to discover anything new or develop solutions to problems. What problems have animals solved? What solutions have animals brought to either their issues or those of humans? If you can only live and build your future on what you see, and if you can only live this way, you will never impact anyone, or bring anything new to the world. In fact, if you live this way, you will be robbing the world of your precious contribution, that would have enriched the lives of others.

Your contribution is needed. Without any meaningful contribution, you have wasted yourself. It is this type of living that creates scarcity, strife, and fights over resources. If one can produce and do what they were supposed to do, there will probably be no injustices, and everyone will celebrate other people's achievements. As we celebrate, people will also celebrate us. If your work is useful, you have the possibility to live forever through your job. The names of those who have made an impact will be written in the history of their profession or area of calling.

I used to say that African civilisation was real until we were unsettled, divided, and somehow destroyed by the west. I have changed my mind. Every human being has a potential for resilience and the ability to change strategies where necessary to readapt and thrive, even after a disaster. As people, we ought to be inspired by developments started elsewhere and to add our fingerprints. We cannot remain the same and become great. We cannot continue to use slavery, imperialism and colonialism as an excuse for our present failure. We know that those events have left fingerprints in our minds. Let us erase those print, since we know what they are, and imprint traits that we want.

A man is made for progress, and change is inherent to life. Therefore, a person's ability to change determines his position at each point of his life. Those who are slow to change will remain behind. Those who are quick and fast will lead the way.

If we are made in God's image, we should always be at work because our "father is always working". Our job should be shaped and guided by our inner thoughts. Being Godlike, we can do great things.

Living in prosperity, ruling the dominion, is our divine mandate. We have jurisdiction and authority to rule the earth. The earth is ours, to transform for better or for worse. Our lives are ours, to improve, destroy or neglect. Our future is in our hands, to decide what we do with it. Nothing can stop us unless we stop ourselves. There are no limits as to what our mind can dream or think of. What can be visualised, what is conceived coherently, can be materialised. Everything was already created before us so that we can decide what to do with it. First, we need to make sense of things that we see, and this is the area of discoveries. **If we cannot make sense of a stone called a diamond, then it is worthless. It is a man that gives meaning and value to natural things.** It is a man that makes physical things useful. There are billions of natural elements in existence today of which we have not yet made sense of their utility, hence their importance. At some point, and progressively, we will uncover the secret of those elements as we learn to understand them.

Discovery is an act of uncovering; unearthing something that already exists, but which had not been to this point considered as having its present valuation. Discovering a thing is understanding its current potential and ability. But what is discovered is not new; it had always been and was always potentially available and awaiting uncovering. We discover that which had always been, but of which we did not know its use or what to do with it.

Discoveries are revealed through our mind's ability to find meanings and the use of existing resources. So, who, without his mind, will make sense of great things in existence? A proper application of our mind leads to a beneficial use of existing resources.

So long as a man fixes his sight on the superficial, it will be impossible for him to grasp the truth. It is practically difficult to make real progress and achieve success without the ability to make sense of what we see. Only our mind helps us to make sense of what we see. The capacity to make sense is a mental function, not a bodily or physical function. A man is a spirit, and his mind helps him to understand his body. The reality and what shapes and determine human progress is within each of us. However, a common man through conditioning and belief in illusions, spends his time looking outwardly for solutions to his life's challenges. Until he turns within, any settlement will only be temporary and limited.

We named animals; we call everything that has so far been discovered, and new discoveries are given names. We can see that man's first preoccupation was not for food. It was to make sense of his environment, and the world he owns as master and ruler. He exercised his intellectual abilities by naming things, and with the same faculties, he expressed the desire for love.

Not only were you created to design and improve this world, you were also set up to be God's representative, and to continue his creative work on earth. Adam communicated every day with God; this means that he had the mind of God and understood the truth, the eternal, the unchangeable. He had an internal spiritual link to God. This communication was spiritual, since the same Bible says that man has never seen God. Moses spoke to God, and yet again, we may ask how? It was a spiritual communication. We are in his image, and he lives within us. We have God's spirit. The pure and genuine- the Holy Spirit.

Man, who has God's attributes, is perfect in potential and in essence, but he ignores his might; he is fooled by a false modesty and claims to be imperfect. This false discourse of man's limitations has been imposed and propagated by fear.

Humans are masters of the earth and designers of their destinies. You, therefore, design your life. You make a conscious or unconscious effort to change it to your liking or not. You can program your subconscious to change your life the way you want it to be.

To succeed, you need to define your destination, believe in your strengths, and not give up. You need to believe in yourself so that where you lack skills, help will arise from unexpected sources. This is the reality of human interactions and mutual interdependency.

When you give up on yourself, others will give up on you, and you end up living a life that is not yours. Followers live other people's lives and follow other people's dreams.

Who sets the limits as to what you can achieve? Only yourself. Up to now, there are no known limits to man's mental ability, and there are no known limits to how far his mind can stretch. He can be inspired and trained to do more, and this should be the aim of any education and training programs. Man's mind is unlimited and illimitable, except by self, even the genus of our time can only use a tiny percentage of their minds. For anyone who uses his mind and applies it correctly will succeed. His spirit will open doors of opportunities, enabling him to move beyond his present circumstances.

There is never a lack of opportunities. There are always possibilities and opportunities for one who spares no effort to look for them. These opportunities are never discovered from outside of self. To find opportunities, we need to be tuned in to the source.

Ben made millions where people found no hope. Ben transformed an environment that was deserted and brought life to the middle of the forest. Beneath the desolate mountains was a hidden treasure, which Ben had the ability to see. It must follow that success is also a matter of how people conduct themselves. Therefore, there must be no injustices that explain the roots of poverty and stagnation, because, even during slavery and colonisation, there were outstanding people of African heritage.

How did they manage to become notorious in such an environment? It must have been their mindset and their ability to think that influenced others and created their passage to fame and success. Their imagination and their ability to turn inwards for solutions helped them. If some people can succeed in all sorts of conditions, it must also follow that poverty or wealth is determined by how people think and act.

How did Joshua lead the Israelites with his disability, after being a slave all his life? (Apparently, Joshua had lost one of his feet). How did he replace Moses who was highly trained and who had never been enslaved? How did a one-footed person lead over three million inhabitants across the desert to the promised land and why was he chosen? We can conclude that his selection as leader was based on other criteria than physical ones. A leader is not the one who is the strongest, but someone with the finest mental attitude. Hence, Joshua's selection as leader was based on his mental attitude. He was the one who believed in himself; after seeing how the land of Canaan was ruled and who ruled it, he was still confident that they could conquer it. Like Joshua, many people have attained mind-blowing achievements. Progress made by humans show that man can do all kinds of things. We just need to more aware of our potential, confident in our abilities, use our mind, and use it well.

Chapter 9

Africa and the Paradox of Lack in Paradise

Despite the world's progress, Africa lags in every area of development. Many African people believe that the West are the cause of their demise. No African takes responsibilities for Africa's lack of progress. This situation is alarming considering the continent's agricultural potential and the variety of its resources.

Africa has around 600 million hectares of uncultivated arable land, representing roughly 60 percent of the global total.

A report by three different U.N. agencies revealed that in 2019, 821 million people will be undernourished in the world of these, 257 million in Africa, with 237 million in sub-Saharan Africa and 20 million in Northern Africa, compared to 2015, when there were 239 million people affected by hunger. This figure was still 20 million higher than the numbers reported in 2008. We can see that Africa is hungrier when the world evolves. African people's conditions have worsened instead of improving and there are no signs of betterment on sight. Why would people be so hungry on a continent with the potential to become a major world food supplier? Why is the number of people suffering from starvation increasing in a world where knowledge and discoveries are in a sharp rise?

African cereal yields, for example, are just over one-third of the developed countries average and have barely increased in 30 years.

One major issue is that as much as 80 percent of Africa's agriculture still depends on rain, not irrigation, and few Africans believe that they can change the situation. Each African is always pointing the finger at others, but never at themselves. This unconscious detachment from the reality implies an admission of inferiority and justifies why they always turn to others for solutions to their problems.

Most of their arguments are that this situation is caused by the West. For them, Africa is so rich that the West will not let it progress. They all believe- and this is true- that Africa is blessed with resources that the world craves. But few know how to locate those resources. There are no serious scientific research centres in Africa to experiment and make discoveries. Almost all the discoveries made in Africa are carried out by the western world. The West discovers these resources, knows exactly what to do with them and puts all its energies and efforts into inventing types of machinery that will facilitate their extraction and transformation. When it comes to investing in the conversion, Africans claim to have no money and the West, naturally, requests significant returns on its investment.

The lack of capital could easily be overlooked if Africans were to work together. What we see is that no government, no wealthy individual, or community want to come together to transform this experience. Everyone thinks that it is someone else's responsibility. The stock exchange could be strengthened to generate the required capital, henceforth the lack of good will and political drive make this impossible. An honest self-evaluation is necessary. However, such is not their priority.

Africans behave as if their contribution was not necessary to the world's problems. Whether in finding the cure for diseases or in doing scientific research, Africa remains elusive. The reality is that a solution to a world problem is also a solution to individual problems. For example, Ben made money solving people's challenges and the solution to people's problems gave him enough income to achieve his life's ambitions.

Poverty is the consequence or result of a lack of insight to problem solving. It is also due to lack of self-belief, and profuse psychological handicaps. **Everywhere there is suffering; there is a spirit of crippled thinking. Where there is scarceness, there is the lack of mindedness and loftiness. Where there is scantiness of opportunities, there is a profusion of unconscious and resigned minds.**

Paradoxically, you can find underground water where there are droughts and a lack of food. Africans lack the courage or willingness to exploit their subsoil water for agricultural purpose.

Consequently, there is always a food shortage, and when there is drought, millions die of hunger, or when there is poor harvest, Africa begs for food from the USA or Europe. Conversely, the USA or Europe does not depend on the rain to feed their people. In some cities of the USA, water is drained, irrigated from hundreds of miles to the area where there is the water shortage.

When projects of a high magnitude are attempted in Africa, they are financed by the West for their interests as an example, 660 miles of pipeline was built from Chad to the coastal area of Kribi in Cameroon to drain oil. If this initiative were not too hard, it wouldn't be too difficult to dig wells or drain water from one part of the country to another for agricultural purpose. The truth is that no one is interested in such projects and there is no interest in carrying out such initiatives by Western investors. This leaves people at the mercy of rain.

Why take a 6000-mile trip to Europe to beg for food when Africa possesses fertile lands and the most generous and mutually helping population, comparable to a communist state? The answer is simple. It is all in the mind. It takes a change of mindset to move away from depending on the rain to using Africa's rivers and streams to produce crops all year long. We know the answer and have the solution. We should stop complaining about being duped and put our efforts to changing the situation. Why complain about lack when the situation is in our hands? There is a choice to be made

Suppose that Africans did not initially know what petrol was and what to do with it. Nowadays, such excuses are no longer acceptable. Today, everyone knows about petroleum and its derivatives. Why are Africans still running to the west to exploit their reserves of petrol once they are discovered?

Despite the availability of crude oil in most Africans countries, refineries are owned and operated by foreign companies. Africans do not refine their own crude oil and have no petrochemical industries, despite being amongst the biggest producers of petrol in the world.

Africans burn gas while exploiting petrol that could be used for electricity, yet they don't have enough power to serve the population.

Africa is full of great rivers. Wind and thunder abound, but unfortunately, wind energy is yet to be transformed into electricity in this part of the world. A village will sing and dance when power is installed, yet they cannot have it continuously due to regular cuts.

Despite the abundance of year-round sun and rivers, Africans can't use this to make electricity to power their houses and industries. It is not that they ignore the importance of these resources or lack the ability to transform them into power. They simply don't care, and this is their mind-set. They just lack the will and motivation to do it. Each person is thinking about their personal benefits. In fact, unconsciously everyone gives up.

Africa produces and exports cotton, but it is a significant importer of textiles from China, Holland and the rest of the world. For generations, Africans have been using the finest imported wax, yet they still don't make it on the continent.

Africans have cattle, crocodiles, and other animals whose skin can be used for leather, but they prefer to eat the skin and buy shoes and handbags elsewhere at an exorbitant price.

Africa grows cassava everywhere, but imports starch from Europe and China.

Africa grows tomatoes and can grow as much as they want, but imports tomato paste. In fact, they are the biggest users of tomato paste in the world.

Africans are amongst the largest producers of coffee and cocoa, but they have no coffee shops or proper chocolate factories.

They import 95% of their chocolate and 99% of coffee and tea from whom they have sold their commodities to, at a million-fold the price they sold their raw products for.

Africa produces rubber, but imports derivatives such as shoes, balloons and tires. A tyre industry does not exist in Africa.

Africa has timber, but imports household furniture from outside the continent.

Africa has gold and diamonds, but few Africans own gold either; in fact, they don't even know how to transform them into fine jewelleries.

About 80% of Africans now have mobile phones but the continent has no satellites, no phone manufactures, and no reputable network distributors.

Africa has all sorts of medicinal plants, yet the population's dying from all types of diseases.

Africa has phosphate, but imports fertilisers.

Africa has uranium; however, it is a stranger to nuclear technology.

Africa's Savannah is gorgeous with sought-after animals, but its tourism is under-developed.

Africa has the most arable land, but its people are dying of hunger.

Africa exports the best footballers in the world but has no professional leagues or decent football stadiums.

Africa builds pipelines to send their gas and petrol abroad, however, the population has no gas connections in their homes.

Iron and bronze from Africa are used to build cars, bridges, and other great structures elsewhere in the world, however, no cars are made in Africa and there are no stunning bridges or fantastic mega structures.

Africa has the most ancient civilisation and precious art; paradoxically, its museums are empty.

Africa has children with the brightest minds and the potential to achieve great things, but there is no appropriate education system to support their inventions or encouragement to further their discoveries.

Here are some facts about the reality in Africa: There are approximately 13 million internally displaced people in the 21 sub-Saharan countries; this amounts to more than a third of the global total of internally displaced people. Nigeria, the Democratic Republic of the Congo, and Sudan have the largest populations of internally displaced people in Africa.

It is estimated that Nigeria alone has between 3 to 5 million internally displaced people; millions of these people are in camps. However, elected people sit in parliaments advocating for how much they should be paid instead of identifying issues affecting their people and solving them. They use their influence to make more money for themselves than serving the country and individuals who voted for them. Parliamentary sessions open with senators; members of parliament's pay negotiation. In Nigeria and other parts of Africa, each member of the parliament has a good car allowance even though there are no car manufacturers. In Nigeria, for example, around 60% of the national budget is for those who run the country- the parliament and ministers- but paradoxically, the country has a struggling army, crumbling administrative buildings, a crippled judicial system and a loose way of collecting taxes, tied by the slowest and most cumbersome regulatory regime.

In most cases, people who have served the country all their lives are forced to pay bribes to obtain their pension. The money the government spend buying cars can be used to build houses for displaced people and creating research centres which focus on improving people's living conditions. Elected members not only use public money for a personal purpose, but the worse thing is that they use it to oppress the population that voted for them and whom they are supposed to defend and protect. Most elected members, such as members of parliament, stay in the capital for their whole term even though they are meant to represent the people in their local communities; instead, they generate money-making ideas for themselves. How can a continent produce sought-after resources and remain deprived? It is a matter of a mindset. A well-known criminal can rally people- even educated people- to support them to obtain power. These educated people will support those criminals to access power, provided they are paid for it. They choose instant gratification instead of thinking about the future of the whole country. They reflect on how to make more money in the present moment while neglecting their long-term job prospects. Students also sacrifice their future for peanuts.

Africans give power to people who create social conditions for their impoverishment. Those wrongly elected erode social and educational systems and fill people's minds with the wrong message. They contribute to disempowering citizens instead of empowering them. They condition them to think they are less worthy and incapable of achieving much. Africa's poverty is not due to its land's poverty. Instead, it is caused by its people's poor mindset. Africa has people with poor minds; Africa's nation is not poor. People think distortedly, wrongly, poorly. They judge poorly, badly, ignorantly. They unconsciously make themselves.

It is not wrong to assert that Africa is not poor; however, the lack experienced by its people is due to a poor application of their thoughts. Africa, the land of the first intelligent man, shouldn't be poor. However, they believe their lives are determined by fate rather than conscious decision-making. They are therefore condemned and reduced to inferior people as result of their mind-set.

Chapter 10

Applying the Principles of Success

Each human being has the potential to be successful. In fact, each person should succeed and achieved beyond measure. No one was created to lack or to suffer. But success is based on fundamental principles: Vision, goals, focus, dedication, determination, action, and a burning desire to bring a contribution to the world. One key ingredient in achieving success is the power of choice supported by a strong will. Success or failure depends on one's choice and the willingness to do so. To make the right thing, each needs to tune-in for guidance and inspiration. It means using his/her mind.

The discovery of self and the achievement of individual purpose is a personal matter. An individual's success has ramifications on a global scale based on a chain of giving and receiving; he who fails to contribute to this chain is a cheat, a fraudster, who lives on borrowed terms. In fact, such people are living "borrowed lives", as already mentioned.

You need to tune in for self-discovery if you want to know your purpose, without which it is hard to make impact on the world. The theory of human possibilism is that nothing is impossible. The theory of human illimitation-ism rests on humans with unlimited potential and ability, hence unlimited power. I contend that there are no limits to what the human mind can perceive and achieve. If there were, these limits are yet to be discovered and tested. With the progress made so far in the world, it has been said that we use less than a tenth of our abilities. When we reach a state where our mind is used to its maximum, we can now start talking about man's limitations, but for now the possibility of our unlimited ability is irrefutable.

Every human being who wants to achieve his potential can do it. It goes the same for Africans.

Africans who have stopped believing in themselves, those who have given up, are betraying themselves. It is their lack of self-belief that unavoidably creates their social conditions of poverty and nothing else. Their conditions are intrinsically linked to how they see themselves and how they think.

If you have almost given up, stand up, pick you your load and move! You can do it: you can be who you want to be and achieve success beyond any man's expectations. You can reach beyond what you thought was possible. You are the creator and master of your destiny. You can decide how and what your future will be if you have a clear picture of what you want. Your legacy is in your hands to design. You can write your history. It is up to you to create and define your life. It is up to you to decide what you want to be remembered for.

Life is supposed to be enjoyed on earth, and no one was made to suffer. The earth is full of everything that is necessary to make life comfortable, to live a pleasant and enjoyable life. If you do not experience a better life here on earth, it is doubtful that you will live it in heaven. You create your heaven through the way you live and act. You can decide whether you will live in paradise or hell;

therefore, if you miss your way on earth, I doubt you will find it in heaven because, if you are indeed connected to the source, if your spirit is in tune, you cannot miss your way. However, you miss your way when you chose the wrong path. Those who are in tune will have a clear direction, including a pathway to success. What you taste on earth will multiply, even increase in a million- "milliontiply"- there when your spirit has left your body. If you are unable to have a glimpse of happiness here on earth, it just means that you are not connected to the source: God. How can you ever reach paradise if you have never been connected to God? If you are a failure here on earth, it may suggest that you have missed the mark.

As you discover your limitless potential and your true essence, you need to tap into it and spring forth. You are a miracle that ignores its true self. You cannot discover it from without; tune in to discover yourself from within. The power of your thoughts, your crucial link to your creator and a purpose-driven life and perfection is in you. You are a spirit and the greater spirit that governs the universe lives in you; just tune in for directions.

As you use what others have done to bring solutions to your problems, you need to be making your contribution. Your actions matter to the world because individual inventions and discoveries belong to all human beings. Each human has the right to this, as well as a duty to contribute. As long as you contribute to the cycle of giving and receiving, you are surely playing your part.

Our potential is unlimited, but only a few people are aware of this ability within despite all human beings made of the same substance. Why are Africans always lagging? Have they understood what is required to achieve freedom and success? These questions are genuine to one who looks around and wonders at the level of disparity amongst humans. Africans claim to be equal, and surely, they are, from the biological point standpoint. However, the difference resides in the way they think and apply their knowledge.

Everyone is equal in essence and potential. However, everyone has their mind, which guides their actions and determines their situation. Everywhere I go in Africa, people expect to be given things, to be helped. They expect others to bring solutions to their problems. Everyone is always claiming not to have the necessary means to achieve something great. Few attempts to do what they are supposed to do. They give up without even starting, and no one tries to team up and work together with others.

Doing the right things in Africa will bring the good results. The proof is that many western businesses are thriving in Africa, and it is not a secret to anyone that Africa is full of opportunities. The right application of the mind results in wise and noble actions. Unwise and high actions bring the same results. Africans' actions create their environment. What we choose to do with our lives makes us either equal, better or less respected and valued than others. This is a bold statement, and many people may not like it. Many people may complain about this declaration. But instead of complaining, I will urge whoever is not happy to do something greater and better than what they are doing now. Once they have accomplished more, they will make up their mind as to whether people's perception of them has changed or not. They will make up their mind as to whether their achievement has made the world a better place or a worse one, and whether their self-esteem has improved or not.

If people are made up of the same substance, inequalities are therefore due to the way each person thinks. Those who think faster and cleverer will always be a step ahead of slow thinkers. Those who use their mind well will always stand out from of the crowd. It is overcrowded at the bottom based on organised social strata. In the realm of the spirit, there are no social strata, and each can make an impact at any time.

Europeans are trained to believe in themselves. Each citizen wants to do something for self, and safeguards are in place to pull up the weakest. Systems exist to support future generations and inspire them to dream big. If such visions are acted upon, other possibilities will follow, and the younger generations will always have more primary goals. When Europeans claim to be great, this may sound zealous, but it stirs up in each citizen the desire to live up to such expectations of greatness, thus forcing people to think creatively to maintain the lead. Unconsciously, systems are in place to further this vision.

Like anyone else, each African has a seed of greatness, potential for creativity and achievement. But false modesty, coupled with the historical conditioning of their mindset, makes them believe that they are less able than others. This self-doubt creates a collective mindset that prevents generations from showcasing their abilities and hinders their drive and motivation for thriving. There is a collective conscience that affects people of the same affinity. Individuals who identify themselves to a particular group will tend to act like them. This is the concept of groupthink. Groupthink, a term coined by social psychologist Irving Janis (1972), occurs when a group makes faulty decisions because group pressures lead to a deterioration of "mental efficiency, reality testing, and moral judgment."

A collective-projective identification influences the way people think. If a behavioural pattern is widespread in a nation, the whole nation will unconsciously adopt it as a norm. For example, Africa has not always been corrupted. The tolerance of such behaviour grew with time, and as it became widespread, it became unconsciously part of citizens' way of life. This is why most people who are part of that system consider it as a norm.

In Africa, corruption and citizens' behavioural pattern can only change through a reprogramming of their mindset. The poor man's spirit can be changed by programming their minds to dream big and to see no limitations as to what one can achieve. This trick will affect the whole nation and pave the way for a future generation of dreamers and achievers. The current system cannot change when one criticises the system but continues to maintain it once he is in charge, to obtain the same personal benefits as his predecessors did. Each should stop perpetuating corruption, mismanagement, embezzlement, and lack of vision.

Human beings copy others and quickly chose options that are less sacrificial. They chose options that require fewer efforts, irrespective of whether they produce good or bad results. Only a few people wanted behavioural patterns that require hard work, abnegation, and self-sacrifice. These people are those who know exactly what they want in life.

A nation should, therefore, forge in its citizens a behavioural pattern that exalts greatness, self-worth, and a desire to achieve.

A belief that nothing is impossible, an excellent moral character and a love of self and the nation. In the same way, people become attracted to those who mimic their behavioural patterns, create affinities and affiliations. For example, drug dealers will always identify where drugs are dealt, even if they are new to an area. Lazy people will easily find others who are lazy no matter where they find themselves; however, if they find themselves surrounded by hardworking people without any possibility of running away, they will at first experience a dramatic shift but eventually start the process of changing their mindset to become a hardworking mindset.

Poor people easily contaminate people around them with their poverty mentality; they find all sorts of excuses to get their allegiance. You hear them say things such as money does not bring happiness. But does poverty bring happiness? Or that money is the root of evil. Poverty is killing millions of people every hour. Money is not a bad thing for society, as there are many ways to put the money to good use. There are schools to be built, homes to be built, hospitals to equip, research centres to fund so they may develop solutions to deal with the challenging issues of our generation and beyond.

Poverty has never been ordained, neither by nature nor by God. Man chooses to live in poverty in exchange for a comfortable ride, as opposed to giving what it takes to get what they are destined for. It is giving up the race, in exchange for taking an easier path. No one will ever reach their purpose if they do not make sacrifices. Reaching your goal may require more readiness, more serving, more training, more studying, more sacrifice and sacrificing the ease of the now to achieve greater goals.

Poverty is an unwise choice for a stupid man. It is the end destination for a fool and a state of mind of a lost sheep. It is a choice. Those who end up with it have done so by volition, by wilfully neglecting their responsibilities towards themselves, and humans. No one can gain alone from their income; every income always goes through a chain to benefit other people. In fact, poor people are those whose present income is taken at once, and they are forced to wander in search of the next small chunk for the next pressing need. Therefore the Bible says that those who have more are given more and for those who have little, the little they have is taken away from them.

People who are only concerned with the "here and now" will be surprised that by the time they sort out their present needs, the next need will be pressing, and they will remain trapped forever in a perpetual struggle to meet daily needs. This short-sightedness causes them to miss the path to permanent victory and freedom. External help can only temporarily alleviate their situation. If they require an ongoing solution to their status, they must find it themselves. The solution is never far away from their reach.

Those who give attention to the steps to take them ahead end up finding the right path to success. Poverty, like success, is indiscriminate. If you follow the laws of success, doors will open for you. Your exit point is your choice. Poverty or richness respond to your call according to the level of your commitment to them. Those who remain in poverty have pledged allegiance to poverty, and those who are successful have signed a long-term contract with prosperity.

Hardworking people, mainly those who believe in themselves, are more likely to succeed if they do not give up and if they know what they want. Individuals who know what they want to ask the right questions to understand what is required of them to get where they want to be. The law of success is the same for all human beings, no matter which country they live in. Therefore, in the desert of Malia or Mauritania, there are millionaires.

In a remote area of each country, you will find successful people. When the law of success is applied in the right way, opportunities avail themselves, no matter where you are. Based on their abilities, people living- for example- in remote villages of Timbuktu have been able to go directly to the USA because of their skills. They have reached their goal, not because they travelled to the USA, but foremost because from Timbuktu they applied the principles of success that opened the doors for their journey to the USA, the ideal geographical location to exercise their talents.

All human beings are delivered into this world to manifest their possibilities and achieve their goal and purpose. However, if they lose their way, the only thing left is to rely on others, and relying on others creates shortage where there should have been abundance.

Chapter 11

Unconscious Limitations and Human Possibilism: A Theory Rooted in Facts

Most people, like the people of Fotetsa, live their lives as if all hope were lost even though they live in a potentially richest land in the world. Africa can totally be transformed if the state invests in changing its citizen's mindset. Most people who have left the continent identify more opportunities back home when they return compared to who remained there. This shift is due to their new mindset, because after leaving the continent, they sharpened their minds against other sharp minds. What they saw somewhere else awakens their dormant potential. Having learned elsewhere, they were able to awaken their mind, and now see what it could not see prior to their exposure to the outside world. The more the mind sees new and good things, the more it can be inspired. The more a mind is exposed to creativity, the more its creative power is brought to life.

Before its transformation, Fotetsa was a desolate land; their youth had left the area and poured into cities in search of better opportunities. They saw nothing extraordinary in their land as their mind had not yet been sharpened. Older people who were left behind sold their land for peanuts. No one, from their great, great, great grandfathers to the younger generation, considered their property as worthy of more than its ability to produce fruits and to house the animals that they hunted for a living. On the other hand, Ben came from far away to fulfil his dream in Fotetsa. He saw in the land, opportunities that the locals were unable to identify. The difference between Ben and other people was that he knew what he wanted and was convinced that he could achieve it anywhere in the world. Other people just wanted to live their ordinary day to day lives. They did not believe they could do anything better than meeting their daily needs. They did not want too much hassle. They wanted a comfortable life, where they could get a job that paid them enough to get by.

Perhaps they did not understand the meaning of opportunities. If they understood it, they would have seen the opportunities, just like Ben did. They unconsciously limited themselves. Unconsciously, many people limit their abilities and possibilities.

From birth, we are conditioned to believe that human beings are imperfect and limited, even though there is no limit to what we can do as masters and rulers on the earth. It is up to us to govern it to our liking. The idea of our imperfection is self- limiting.

If we set out to do something, only the sky will be the limit. Since there is no wall and no flooring to the heavens, we can go as high as we wish and as wide as we chose. In fact, we can go on and on and on; there are no limits. Each discovery will unfold the next one, and so forth.

When we say the sky is the limit, we are in fact saying that there are no limits because the heavens we see are just a blurry image of the clouds. The position of the cloud depends on the location from where we look, and the weather conditions now we are looking. There are days when the sky seems so close, but equally, there are days that it seems very far away. But, behind the clouds is space, and behind the clouds, there is unlimited height and depth, unlimited width, and infinite length. So, it is with human abilities.

Although there is no limit to what we can achieve, our blurry vision makes us think that we have reached our full potential even when we are still at the beginning of our efforts. If we push further, we will discover another dimension to our abilities and potential.

What we think that we cannot do is possible; conversely, everything we perceive as possible can be achieved. Our possibilities depend on our will power to surpass the present. The sky we see is just an illusion, created by the clouds. So, our ability to make anything depends on the image we project into our subconscious. A distorted image will project a distorted view of what we believe attainable. Our false imagination or our illusions determines the heights we can attain, thereby setting the limits to our potential.

To do anything great or grand, you need to have such a conviction of yourself and your ability to do it. You must believe with all your heart that you will do what you were made to do. "Be careful how you think; your thoughts shape your life." (Proverbs 4:23 TEV). The change of mindset is more important than the change of circumstances. When the mind has formed the habit of holding confident, happy, and fruitful images, it will not be easy to create different patterns.

William Walker Atkinson said that if "the body subjects to the control of the mind, one may change the environment, 'luck', circumstances, by positive thoughts taking the place of negative thoughts". For him, "I Can, and I Will" attitude will carry one forward to success that will seem miraculous to the man on the "I Can't" plane.

Each human being is a creative power. Each has unlimited ability to create, imagine and invent things, and by so doing, to recreate his history. What you make of the world is up to you. Therefore, every human being, like every society, must choose the type of values that they articulate and promote. The values that you promote become what you are known for. If you want to remain where you are, it is up to you. If you want to drive a moto taxi or an aeroplane, it is up to you. If you want to live in a rabbit hut or to write books, it is up to you. It is not so much about how hard you work. It is about how determined and how far you can stretch your mind.

So, why do some people think that material conditions determine man's social conditions? This vision is a materialistic view that limits an individual from stretching their minds. Quality thinkers are quality people, and quality thinkers cannot beg. A quality thinker will, through his ability to think right, find the right solution for his problems. Abundant solutions bring abundant wealth, and poverty suggests scarcity. Therefore, quality thinkers cannot be poor.

Poverty is the result of one's inability to think correctly. Some people forfeit their right to contribute to the development of society, in exchange for instant gratification: meeting their pressing needs. They want to relax, not think hard enough, not study, not try to fix things when they continuously go wrong, not attempt to achieve anymore once they have reached a certain age. One final push could be the last push to glory.

Human beings are potentially perfect and can be effectively perfect if they want and believe it possible. The Bible says that "you ought to be as perfect as your father". Jesus would not say this if perfection were not attainable. Man's imperfection is due to his body; however, man is not his flesh, he is a spirit. The things that are seen are temporal, and the things that are not seen are eternal. The body is temporal and imperfect. However, the spirit is eternal and can be perfect. If it constantly contemplates perfection. Man, being a spirit, is perfect- in principle.

Spiritually, humans can do anything; they can achieve any project, however warranting their earthly manifestation requires imagination, dedication, and abnegation. Instead of bowing to our physical urges always, it is better to put an emphasis on developing our spiritual abilities. The spirit can bring great benefits to the body, and it is naturally what it should be. Each person's spirit determines the quality of their life; this reflects on their body, well-being, health and longevity. It is crucial to winning the war against the physical limitations to bring about the manifestation of spiritual fruits.

When you start to think about how powerful you are, you will understand that you are a miracle.

Do not give up; each challenge is an enfoldment for your real self. Each challenge is necessary, either voluntarily or not; it is the way to veer away from the wrong path or better, yet to head towards an unknown destination where you will understand why the challenges were necessary. Many people become discouraged and give up in the middle of difficulties; as a result, they fail to reach their desired destination.

Every man's work is a signature of his life. What you do determines who you are and where you are going. What you do determines what you are known for, and what your family will become known for. Thoughts of greatness create a state of greatness. Achieving greatness without great ideas is difficult. People with a will to succeed, cultivate these thoughts and never give up because they know that they are destined to succeed. Ben could not give up because he was aware that he was intended to become great.

"The things that are seen physically are temporal, and the real is the realm of unseen things" (Corinthians 4:18). The spirit realm is greater than the physical realm, and there is no limit to a spiritual realm. You are already like God and therefore you are already great you are now aware, act like it.

Chapter 12

Poor Man; Or, the Syndrome of Borrowed Identity

Many people live on borrowed identity as they spend their life moving aimlessly following other people or current trends. Instead of finding their own way, they live other people's dreams. They live a life of followers, under the pretence of seeking opportunities. Although some opportunities can be linked to a geographical location or specific sector, it's hard to make the most of any by accident. Prepared individuals, who are clear about what they are looking for, will identify and jump on opportunities that open to them. **Opportunities are useless, unidentifiable, unrecognisable to an ignorant.**

There were many people in Melong at the time that Abada moved from his village to that part of the country in search of a better life. However, not many villagers moved with him; neither did every inhabitant of Melong benefit from the roadwork program. Although the project offered an excellent opportunity to many, there were still unemployed people living in the city who did not identify road building as worthwhile. Abada's death provided an opportunity for Sekou, and when he subsequently moved to Mengang, he had a clear game plan: Take any job offer that came his way, regardless of what people thought about him. He had a humble and prepared heart, and he kept believing and working hard, even in the jungle where he could have easily given up. Focus and self-belief were the keys to his success.

This trait can be found in Ben who believed in his abilities and would not rest until he achieved his goal. The attainment of targets brings freedom that only a few people experience. With financial freedom, Ben was delivered from worries, from needs, free from lack, and consequently, free to go where he wanted in the world. He could now travel around the world, and he could afford anything he wanted. Greater freedom is made possible by financial freedom. True freedom is connected to wealth and spiritual stability in one way or another. You attain mental stability when you know your true self, and when you are connected to your true self, knowing your life purpose. You discover the self through a connection to the immutable. If you are wealthy with a spiritual balance, you are free, and you can choose where to go, and where to live in the world. Tough visa conditions are only for poor people.

If you are poor, you have limited choices. You have limited choices on where you can live, where you can go, what you can do, what you can eat, and to some extent, who you can see, and what you can say. People have died at sea whilst trying to reach countries where they expect to be better off. These people did not have to risk their lives if they had access to what they wanted, or if they were financially able.

Despite the abundance of opportunities in Africa, millions of Africans live in destitution, because they have not been trained to identify opportunities around them. Most training and educational programs are inadequate and unable to stimulate young Africans' curiosity, inquisition, imagination, and creativity. They are not trained to believe that their environment could offer them the best opportunities. All their training and examples are based on the western world, which unconsciously makes them feel that there are no potential solutions, let alone opportunities, at home. They are educated to get a job and not to create jobs, and when they find no jobs at home, the easiest solution is to job hunt elsewhere.

The situation is exacerbated by the lack of emphasis on scientific research. The state gives no room to research and innovation but spends half of the national budget on buying ready-made solutions, which become obsolete even before they are acquired and before their implementation. They train solutions users, instead of training solution bringers. They have completely misunderstood the role of education.

Each country in the world needs intelligent people, but those who manage to thrive intellectually in Africa are lured away by the western world. They know that brighter minds will identify opportunities in trivial things to keep them ahead. People who can think creatively bring a solution to problems.

If you have not made a difference either through the quality of your mind or through your ability to create wealth, you are a liability.

Every country and every government want to attract either rich people or brighter minds, and a rich and an intelligent mind will identify premium solutions to problems, which will attract wealth accumulation. **Mediocre minds are a synonym of deprived people and deprived people are a source of challenges for the state. No government wants poor people, as they pay neither taxes nor generate any income for them. Instead, they create additional expenditures.**

Poorer countries remain more deprived and deficient because the little they have been investing in social infrastructure yields no returns. They keep investing in educational systems that only created dependent individuals- solution users instead of solution bringers- a failed education system fails future generations and fail the state.

When you have no income, you have few choices, but with financial freedom, you have a whole raft of options. For example, when Ben arrived at Leke, he had no choice about where to live, perhaps what to eat, but later, his wealth opened up doors and opportunities and options. Ben's financial freedom gave him and his family a multidimensional freedom. They may be living in a country where freedom is expensive, but they can afford it. They can move to where they will feel more comfortable when they desire to do so. When you have financial freedom, your mind is free, and you can treat your body with care. The better your body feels, the happier you are.

We already know that the quality of our thoughts can change the quality of our life and that poverty is created by a state of mind rather than a state of the land. We also argue that freedom from lack can bring about freedom of movement. In other words, **poverty is like a sentence - when you are poor, you are probably condemned to eat what you may not want to eat, to live where you wouldn't have lived, and to accept what you are given. When you are poor, you don't live the type of life you want.** If you are poor, you are indebted to the state, to society, and to yourself; your life does not belong to you. Someone may ask how it is possible to be indebted to oneself? The answer is: you owe yourself a treat, a good holiday, a comfortable home, better clothing, etc. For the state, it is simple. The state makes money from its citizens, and if you cannot pay your contribution to the system, you are creating a deficit.

In Europe, for example, during every electoral campaign, the issue of how to deal with poor people always divides opinions. Some people claim that poor people are costly to the system and the economy because they live on other people's hard work. Others invite those who are better off to be more sympathetic to the poor, arguing for a generous package to support them. The reality is that someone pays for the cost of poverty.

How do you feel when people are debating about you, without your input? How do you feel when people are deciding on which type of house you may live in, how many rooms you are entitled to, where you should ideally be living, without asking your point of view?

Many poor people think that they have no choice; but those who normally have little choice are the mentally disabled, those who are ill. As an able individual, you have a choice. Your situation is in your hands. Social mobility is not an empty concept. It is the right word to describe people who are no longer content with the little life they are living, and who have decided to move up the ladder. It describes those who have managed to increase their income, thus increasing their scope of choices, their position, and their freedom.

When you begin to have more income, more choices start to open to you. Your experiences will expand. The more you have, the better you can control your own life. But, if you are poor, you are living someone else's life. If you are poor, you are living on borrowed and imposed terms.

If you are poor, you are not alone, but this is not a good thing; it only means that you have joined the crowd of those who have abandoned their birth right of freedom, achievement and prosperity to fate. You have resigned, and this is a shame. You have the same attributes as any other human being. You can achieve what other people have attained, and if you think that you cannot, you are implying that some people are superior in nature to others. Are they really?

There are billions of people on this planet who, instead of living and doing what they were destined to do, spend their days, nights, and years aimlessly. They follow official discourses. Most people on this planet are followers. They follow what they don't understand; they follow what they don't agree with as if they had no choice, and they continue to follow what they are asked to follow throughout their lives.

Those who are better off invent official ideologies. They team up with the state to increase the number of followers. What the state and the better off present as facts are their facts, based on their personal experiences, and their worldview, which nonetheless becomes a reference point for the followers- the poor.

What is official certainly does not represent everyone's view. The official programme of a country is only an ideology. The official vision of a conglomerate is someone's ideology. Followers are like fans. Sometimes fans want to become like the people they so admire. Fans are followers. The world is full of fans and those they fancy make their living off them.

The official discourse does not represent your vision. It represents the conceiver's vision. When you follow and spend your life pursuing other people's vision, you will remain a follower for life. If you want to succeed, you must be yourself. You must pursue your dreams, your vision and purpose. Only through pursuing your vision can you contribute to society and exercise your right to be free.

When you spend your life following someone else's dream, you are living that person's life and dream. When you are living an imposed life from without, you are thus living a borrowed life. Billions of people have been living a borrowed life since their first day on earth. The impact of borrowed living is reduced when the system finds a way to filter down part of the wealth to the poor. When most of the population has access to food, medical care, and education, they will find some time and breathing space, to tune in to find better solutions if they so wish. They could, at some point, make a conscious effort to detach themselves from the official discourses and find the way to self-discovery by themselves. It explains why Europe and the USA continue to thrive. Their welfare system gives people some breathing space to reflect. The high number of achievers in these countries inspires others to dream big.

It is quite easy to be a follower, a number-adder, a user and consumer, or a receiver for your whole life. It is easy to spend your entire life trying different things that others have taught you, without thinking about discovering the truth about yourself, your worth, your purpose, your destiny. Your mind is yours. You have no shared mind. Likewise, your dreams are yours. You alone know them. You can find the way to make them happen.

To be yourself and to be free, you need to make a personal effort. You have a mind to think. You are a thinking being, and you have the creator's mind. You need to tune in for answers. You need to ask for guidance, with faith; listen to the still, but wise voice within you, which is saying that you have so much to give to the world in the area of your calling. This voice reminds you every day that you are a unique person; that you are special and a miracle.

You should not be poor. If you are, it is a sign that you have missed your way. If you are struggling, you are still on the wrong path. If you are struggling, you are probably a follower, out of your destiny. You hold the key to your success. If you are poor, you have failed to write your own chosen amount on the blank cheque that you have been given at birth. The sum of money you can write to yourself is unlimited. God's supply is endless, inexhaustible.

Provided you press in for the demand, not out for the way imposed. You will discover yourself when you start to ask yourself what your purpose is. If you regularly ask this question, you will receive an answer. Ask the question with courage and apply the results.

God lives inside of you. He is waiting for you to ask questions. Listen to the answers; they may be brief and apparently trivial, but when you follow them, they will lead you to the next action until your purpose unfolds.

From their experience in the forest, Ben understood that man could change his life, and make of it what he wished. Some people call this optimism; the ability to see opportunities in challenging situations. Ben's motto was: "Man can temporarily experience scarcity, but when it becomes permanent, it is not normal".

The first human being on earth was a businessman; he discovered the formula for solving personal issues through his ability to think. Left alone in nature, he had to find solutions for living. He had to control nature. He had this ability, and he somehow triumphed. We inherited discoveries. We must create a chain that other people benefit from.

The first human on earth had to use his mind to subdue and overcome circumstances and difficulties. He did not have any welfare systems, or the international community to provide aid. The first humans were self-employed, explorers, inventors, and researchers. Like the first humans on earth, Ben did not go around begging or seeking help. He knew that he was able to do as he wished. In fact, he acted as if he had no choice. He focussed on his dream; the meaning of his life depended on it, and he achieved his goal despite the difficulties.

Like our ancestors, each of us has a choice as to whether to brave challenges by forcing his way through the winding slopes of life or to give up and resign to fate. Despite having been given a blank cheque at birth, some people are not able to write it to themselves. This is common in parts of the world where poverty and hunger affect millions of people. Refusing to think deeper, these people still want to use the same rudimentary tools that have been in use for hundreds of years and used by their ancestors. It is a concern when people do not take advantage of discoveries made elsewhere, or when they do not seek to improve on what they have inherited from their ancestors. This observation reveals that, for these people, there is a spirit of stagnation. Anything that does not change, regresses. Stagnant water will reduce in size over time.

A population that does not find new ways of doing things becomes obsolete and incapable of advancing. This attitude is not typical for a thinking being it goes against the nature of thinkers. The solution to any issue is never far from a problem; it can be found through thinking deeply. He who cannot find a solution to his problem is he who refuses to think hard enough. The higher the challenge, the greater the ability of the challenged to find a solution.

People who are anonymous are those who are not doing what they are supposed to do, and for this reason, they are not living the life they were meant to live. Perhaps they are doing someone else's job. Living someone else's life is a result of laziness. Apathy means a disposition to remain inactive or inert. Each person must overcome their inertia and get back to work. Laziness is the trait of being idle, out of a reluctance to work, a failure to be active because of a lack of initiative or ambition. Being relaxed and looking for easy activities. Laziness is an attitude of apathy and inactivity in practice.

We see in this stupidity a wilful attempt to avoid commitment and effort. Any person who cannot make efforts to produce something will still need to meet his physiological needs to remain alive. He will still need to eat and if we just eat what we find, who will supply? Who will replenish the stock? The only way we can maintain the supply and replenish is by producing more.

Those who find useful solutions will not lack financial or material benefits. Solving other people's problems provides people with income to solve their problems. It is therefore clear that a poor person is not bringing any solutions to any individual's problems.

A poor person is not providing any useful solution to any human problems. He is not impacting anyone's life. His life is not helpful. He is not contributing to society. He is hiding, refusing to help anyone, but taking from everyone without giving anything in return. He can only receive the crumbs. But if he had something useful to offer, he would obtain a premium for his contribution and his premium would help him to make a decent living out of his contribution. It is as simple as that. So, a poor man or a poor woman is running away from their responsibilities.

- Why wouldn't you lack if you live on other people's dreams? African, answer!
- Why wouldn't you be poor if you only live and rely on other people's thoughts? African answer!
- Why wouldn't you be poor if you live in other people's brain children? African answer!
- Why wouldn't you be poor if you can't be bothered to know the potential of the resources of your land? African answer!
- What would you do with your petroleum if you can build any car to use it on? Africa answer!
- What would you do with your petroleum if you cannot do not have the secret for refining it? African answer!
- What will you do with your diamonds, gold, iron, cobalt, phosphate, uranium, zinc, manganese, etc. if you do not know what they are used for and what to do with them? Africa answer!

- Do you have any choice than to sell your resources at an imposed price? I think you do. First, you need to find out how you can process them yourself. Your unprocessed resources bear no added value.

- Why haven't you tried, since you knew the importance of such commodities, to exploit and transform them by yourself? African answer!

You find an easy way to meet your present needs, yet you cannot be satisfied because you do not know the process of generating revenues from what you already have. If your revenues come from someone else, remember that the person knows the formula to generate extra revenues, over and repeatedly. You cannot be bothered to find solutions to your problems.

You cannot free yourself if you let other people do the thinking for you. The solutions they find are for themselves and not for you. You are a master of your destiny and have to discover your future by yourself. Africa; reflect, think, and plan!

There is no secret to success, although some people believe there is. To succeed in any endeavour requires tenacity, devotion, commitment, and conviction; also, one must have faith that the destination is reachable. If any, the secret to success is always to find a way to improve yourself, no matter where you are or what position you hold. You must learn all you can and maintain an intellectual curiosity. Surely this is how it works.

The discovery of radio waves led to X-rays, media frequencies, television, satellite, to the Internet and so on and on. Had we stopped at the discovery of radio waves, other things would never have been discovered or invented. We are still on the move, and the world is still under construction. The best discoveries are yet to come. You can be the one to discover the next cure for cancer. You can be the person to make a discovery on how to make people grow taller or to find a solution to one of the world's challenges.

With all that has already been discovered, why are hoes still being used in Africa for farming? Why are you still using machetes when we have engines? It is possible to create new tools using existing inventions. Last year, you used the same instruments and were hungry the whole year. You have not learned a lesson. This year, you are starting your season with the same old tools, using the same old techniques. You can be confident that hunger is looming, just like last year.

No successful mind should stop midway. Successful people always want to give more, to do more and to solve more problems. Therefore, they are so successful. Their success comes from their ability to solve people's problems. Solutions generate a profit because they add value.

To be successful, you should think about how much is possible and how much more can be done. This mental attitude will attract others to you. Your ability to find useful solutions to peoples' problems will ensure that others notice you. Ben was such a man, and therefore he was known beyond Dschang and Fotetsa.

People like Ben are quality thinkers, who use their mind wisely. Ben's qualities and abilities can be found in every human being. Successful people possess the same qualities as others. The difference resides in their minds- how they choose to use their minds. The difference is that poor people do not make use of their abilities, and successful people stretch their abilities.

There was no reason why Dschang could not become as great as London. London is great regarding the number of individuals who live in the city as well as its great features. Still, the people who run this town have not stopped thinking about how to improve it even more. Across the world, people have shown the human mind's ability through their achievements. Changes in many countries have also demonstrated that wealth can be obtained in dry lands as well as in coastal areas. It depends on how people use their minds in each field.

With unlimited mental possibilities, man can achieve practically anything. The possibilities are so vast that science cannot tell if there are any limits to man's spiritual possibilities. Time and time again, we witness inventions that are unbelievable. They did not start with our generation, and will not stop with us, but we have a responsibility toward future generations. Our contribution matters.

We are marvelled by the Egyptian pyramids and Stonehenge. It is as if men communicate with each other, across time and space, without even knowing it, inventions, and discoveries in one part of the world affect people's lives in other regions. Hence why, like a piece of the jigsaw, one man's discovery, without prior arrangements, compliments another man's, as if one part were waiting for the other one to complete the picture. Equally, one innovation is quickly improved upon by another person for the benefit of humans in general.

The law of wealth creation, the laws of personal achievement and the law of nature are available to all and can be uncovered by whoever seeks them. Each person should be useful to the world, but most people don't fulfil their duty. Most people fail to understand why they were sent here on earth. No one is born by mistake or by accident. Each person is born with a potential. Children born to the same parents develop different personalities, abilities, and achievements. This difference is due to their preferences, what they like and what they are passionate about.

One brother, perhaps even more privileged at birth than the other, grows up to become stupid and a beggar, and the other, born under unfavourable conditions, becomes a world-changer. Two brothers, perhaps twins, born on the same day, to the same parents, end up developing different personalities, talents, and skills. One may become poor and the other rich. The difference resides in the way they think. I am convinced for this reason more than any other assumptions. We have been talking about Ben throughout this book. Ben was the third son of the family, not the last. Ben made a conscious decision to succeed, while his brothers remained with their father and achieved less.

Every human comes into the world with great potential. They only need to tune in to identify their purpose. External factors can inspire each person's destiny, but they need to turn inwards to find their real purpose.

Only from within, can we discover ourselves. Only from within, can we see our real potential. External factors are important, but true revelation and discovery of self is a mental exercise and an introspective exercise. Each is meant to become something worthwhile, something unique and perfect. Each can live in abundance. No one is born with a signature for failure. No one is born with a ticket to poverty, even though he may be born into a low-income family. Nothing condemns or castigates a poor person to remain impoverished. He can move above his inherited situation and conditions.

Every human has traits of perfection and the ability to be perfect. The Bible says, "Be ye perfect as your heavenly Father is perfect" (Matthew 5:48).

We can look at different versions of the Bible to understand that there are no limits to human nature as far as perfection is concerned:

New International Version: "Be perfect, therefore, as your heavenly Father is perfect".

New Living Translation: "But you are to be perfect, even as your Father in heaven is perfect".

Man is perfect in potential and in nature, but false humility has made people think that they are limited, imperfect and unable to achieve what our weaker mind calls impossible. There are undreamed possibilities in ordinary citizens. Sometimes we may judge others as less able, perhaps due to their appearance, but everyone has the potential to achieve great things.

How will the world know your potential if you do not use it? The only way to win the world's respect is by living and fulfilling your purpose. It is possible for every individual to discover their potential. The reason why people fail to identify and activate their potential is due to their distraction, and their mistake of finding solutions outside of themselves.

The truths men perceive by inspiration are thoughts held in their mind. If they were not thoughts, people could not understand them, for they would have no existence. They could not exist as ideas unless there is a mind for them to exist in, and a mind can be nothing else than a substance which thinks. Descartes described a man as "a substance whose essence and nature is to think. A man is a thinking being. He makes things happen through his ability to think". This is the foundation of his knowledge and power. Descartes showed the necessity of becoming spiritually awakened. A man should be able to hear himself, revealing deeper truths about himself. An unthinking person is a victim of circumstances. People have prayed to gain an insight into a situation. Through prayers, people have been able to understand what to do in stressful situations. A poor person who has prayed earnestly for a solution to his problem, may suddenly, by a revelatory insight, understand what to do, and when he follows, he will find his way to success.

Jesus was a champion in tuning-in and in praying. He said clearly that each human being could do greater things than what he did. He suggested that he was linked to the eternal, to the source of all knowledge: God the father. "I do what I see the Father do", he said. This means that he was linked directly to God's mind. "The Father shows all things to the Son". If any man has the will to do the will of God, he shall know the truth. My teaching is not my own, but his that sent me. "You shall know the truth, and the truth shall make you free". "The spirit shall guide you into all truth". You have a solution within, and you need to be linked to the source of knowledge to identify that solution for which the world is craving. Like Jesus, we are the sons and daughters of God, and we can therefore also do what we see the Father do.

Michel Ngue-Awane

Chapter 13

Think Your Way Out of Poverty

Ben had added a private jet and a helicopter to his precious possessions. Despite never travelling outside of his country, he was well informed about what was going on around the world. Ben was well known beyond his country and his continent and sought after by people and companies that targeted wealthy clients. His employees came from all over the continent. He could afford whatever he wanted. Now, because he was financially free and as the boss, he did not need to do things by himself. He hired experts to advise him and to help him achieve his goals.

He did not, as you may imagine, know how to fly an aeroplane. So, he hired the best pilots in his

237

country to fly his plane. He wanted to visit many places across the continent as he had heard so many stories of suffering. He had seen a lot of suffering in his own country, but he wanted to understand why hunger, pain and misery were gripping Africa. He wanted to figure out what made some people so prone to suffering. He wanted to live with the locals in each African country he visited to understand if there was a common trait among poor people. He was seeking answers to the following questions: Is poverty a matter of choice or inheritance? Why were Africans so poor? Was it because they lack the will to work hard or was it because the world was unjust?

Using the geographic knowledge, he gained through his education, he decided to visit the following countries: Ghana, Burkina Faso, Malia, Togo, Ivory Coast, Cameroon, Gabon, Democratic Republic of Congo, Kenya, Ethiopia, South and North Soudan, Central Africa Republic, Chad, Senegal, Niger and Nigeria.

His general view about these countries gave him a good understanding of Africa. He was convinced that Africans were doing something wrong. If the problem was limited to one country, it was understandable, but if every African country had similar problems, there must be similarities regarding behavioural patterns and approach to problems solving.

Poverty in Africa, according to Ben, must have deeper causes than what is suggested by the superficial discourses. The widespread opinion is that African people are poor because their resources have been confiscated. Some people argue that even some European countries have been dominated and occupied by others but have somehow recovered and have overcome poverty. China for example has suffered also wars and famine at some point, and they are emerging. Each country had experienced some domination or catastrophe in some way and most western countries, despite their past have recovered. Why is Africa stagnant?

A country is made up of people, and an empty land cannot develop without any human action. An area is developed by the individuals who live there and if some parts of the world are more developed than others, the difference is down to the way each group thinks, behaves, and acts. This argument reinforces the idea that poverty is in mind and not in the land. It is not a coincidence that over 80% of African countries face the same problems. Africa's suffering, hunger, misery, and poverty may not be down to external factors. The causes of Africa's problem should have found in the continent and traced, perhaps in its people's minds and way of life. Ben was eager to test this theory as he journeyed across the continent.

From his personal experience, He was convinced that Africans were able to overcome poverty and hunger. During his history lessons, he was touched and profoundly affected by the treatment of Africans. He learned about great empires and great civilisations, great wars, the slave trade, great countries, great revolutions. In fact, history has proven how wonderful and equally stupid human beings have been. The most amazing thing was that wars and slavery were crazy ideas triggered by individuals. Slavery was inhumane and stripped people of their dignity. Could this be the origin of African people's inferiority complex? Were there any other causes than just a lack of achievement in Africa? Ben was convinced that history of colonisation, exploration and slavery had a role to play, but he wanted to understand other hidden causes, and most importantly how to change African's mindset.

Ben would also test a popular idea which suggests that some nations want to dominate the world and force others to follow them using all means possible. Perhaps this second theory coined well with his idea of the alienation and unconscious conditioning of Africans. If this is the case, people will need to learn new ways of thinking. Their agility and ability to think creatively will make them more resilient and proactive, and this attitude will enable them to shift from poverty to abundance.

Thirdly Ben wanted to know how Africa benefited from selling his its children into slavery. He did not understand why such a vast and historically great continent, with great kings, suddenly disintegrated. He did not know why people continued to beg for food, despite the continent's fertile soil and arable lands. They must be doing something wrong. If he were able to succeed against all the odds, everyone else could succeed. If he went from being a nobody to a well-known figure in his country, others were able to do the same. Ben was proud of being African but deeply unhappy about the presiding and alarming state of lack in the continent.

Over three thousand years ago, the continent had a thriving economy, with long-distance trade and the ability to manipulate stone, clay, and metals to a sophisticated degree. Some great kingdoms and empires existed across Africa from the 5th century through to the 16th century. Common to each of these great empires was an extensive trans-Saharan trade with the North, with a large standing army and a very efficient and effective taxation system.

In the 13th century, Mali rose under the leadership of the Malinke Sundiata Keita to become renowned throughout the Arab world for its wealth and learning. In Burkina Faso, the Mossi became renowned, and the Moro Naba ruled a vast kingdom with proud people and warriors. In present Benin, the Abomey were organised and almost invincible. In Cameroon, the Bamouns, with Njoya the Sultan, built a great civilisation and incredibly organised systems with their language and alphabet. We cannot forget the Bamileke with various chiefs such as Fotetsa, Foreke, Foto, or the Douala and Ewondo with their well-known Kings, and so on.

It is astonishing how people who accomplished such great exploits suddenly became phlegmatic and beggars. It is not a mystery, however, that the situation had become so. Someone must have played a trick with African people's minds. Someone somewhere managed to bring them down and kept them there. Not only by force but certainly by playing mind tricks on them.

We can see that during the hegemony of Africa, no one talked about the scarcity of poverty in the continent. There are no records of poverty, famine pre-slavery and pre-colonisation. It is a clear suggestion that Africa must have been prosperous. In fact, a record of abundance, and advanced food preservation techniques can be found in Egypt, where there were seven years of famine across the globe but during this period, Egypt supplied food to the world. Example Jacob and his family came from Israel to buy food in Egypt. It is at this time that the Israelites settled in Egypt and subsequently became slaves for 440 years. This happened over 5000 years ago, not 500 years. These examples illustrate how great Africa had been in the past. Where have all these kingdoms and great people with their knowledge and advance technology gone?

Do their descendants lack resilience and the ability to follow their forefathers' footsteps? Is it too hard to uncover and transcend the mind tricks others play on them? I am sure Africans have a choice. They can still become great if they want. They can insulate their minds against the poisonous toxins of the dominant force. They don't have to follow the world and the development in which they are strangers. They can find their unique strengths and work on them to become the leaders.

Ghana and other West African countries are fascinating for their history of great kingdoms. Ironically, the controversy that took place in this region is astonishing. How did such great empires fall under slavery and imperialism so quickly? Why did powerful kingdoms like the Ashanti start selling their children into slavery? Why haven't they recovered till now?

Despite Ghana having great kingdoms, they were significantly affected by the slave trade. This corrupt and shameful practice claimed more Africans in this region than anywhere else on the continent. Why did such great kingdoms facilitate the slave trade instead of preventing it? The cause of this again can be traced to the minds, not the land.

Encouraged by his achievement, Ben was determined to understand and possibly transform his people's experience. His dream now extended beyond Dschang and Fotetsa. His dream was for the whole continent to be free from poverty forever. He was ready to discover the continent, travelling throughout Africa, where he would live with people of different cultures and countries to understand their mindset. He had been preparing this great journey of discovery for a long time and was now ready to start. His private jet was ready for him. His pilots were ready and waited for him.

It was the very first time he had flown in his aeroplane. His heart was pounding as he walked through the corridors of Dschang Airport. His internal organs thumped against his chest as his assistant dragged his bag along the carpet floor. The airport was nothing compared to his castle. However, its structure was nonetheless imposing.

As he walked into the VIP departure lounge, he glanced up and sighted a sign directing him to the board of the plane. His body could barely hold itself together with the excitement of embarking on a dream journey. Not only had he bought a plane, but he was also going to board it for the first time. Him, this little nobody man, from. He could not tell exactly where he was from. Would he say Mengang, Sekou, Melong or Santchou? Santchou was another name of Saa'Nzok, the birthplace of his grandfather. Where was he really from? He concluded that he was where he felt comfortable and, since he was comfortable at Fotetsa by Dschang, he was from there. Fotetsa was now his home, and his descendants will be from there unless, like him, they chose to settle elsewhere.

As he proceeded, a swarm of people walked around him, each following the sign to their flight. Ben continued, as he treasured knowing that one of his lifetime goals was now inevitably about to occur.

He remembered the dream he had as a child in Mengang when he saw himself flying. Now, it was no longer a dream. It was a reality. Ben had always believed and was convinced that he could if he wanted, do anything he wanted to do in life. Though it has not always been a smooth ride, his determination and focus had confirmed that nothing was impossible to he who believes.

From the day he became conscious of his being and his presence on earth, he knew that one day, he would fly. That he would own castles, mansions, yachts, aeroplanes, hectares of lands, universities and private schools, hospitals, and clinics.

He had now worked his way up the ladder of great people in his country and was counted amongst the richest in the world. However, up to this point, he had not yet travelled beyond the borders of his country.

Ben was heading to Ghana. Although he could afford the most expensive hotels in the world, he wanted live with low-income families in Ghana. Ben would not disclose anything about himself and will disguise himself and not reveal his real name either. This was the best way to understand people and their way of thinking.

Less than three hours after boarding the plane, Ben landed at Kotoka International Airport, Accra. Once at the airport, his jet was parked in a private area of the airport he had rented for the duration of his stay in Accra. His assistants went each to their hotels, all paid for by Ben. He zoomed toward the city in a taxi that dropped him in the middle of the town. He started looking for a host; it didn't take long before he found Kweku returning from his work in the mines. Ben explained that he didn't have enough money for a hotel room and had nowhere to stay. In this part of the world, people were very hospitable. Kweku did not hesitate to take him to his home without even asking his name and where he came from.

Ben and his host proceeded downhill until all they could see was the sea; however, just before the sea was a slum where Kweku lived. He opened the door of his home and invited his guest in. Akwaaba—meaning welcome.

As they entered the house, Ben noticed condensation sliding its way down the narrow windows of the house, which was lazily erected by the sea banks. It left behind a ribbon of smooth, murky darkness. The mismatched materials used to make the house served as decoration. Inside, 12 drenched bodies sought refuge from the relentless onslaught of rain that had started to fall, making the atmosphere suffocating.

In one corner, a pale figure was pushing up parts of the roof, which threatened to cave in beneath the weight of rain. It was precisely the middle of the bed that Kweku's parents occupied. The shaky hand, despite being busy holding up the roof, managed to shake Ben's, before returning to work quickly. Despite not knowing Ben, they were very happy to be his host. The handshake reassured Ben that he was welcome.

After almost half an hour, Kweku's mother, who was known as Nana Abena, lost the battle against the pouring rain and had no choice but to receive a good amount of water on her bed.

The house was comprised of three rooms, which hosted over 12 people. Despite being overcrowded, they found no problem welcoming Ben to their home. They were used to it. With Ben's arrival, this small house would now host 13 people.

Kweku was a young man in his teens. He had completed his A levels just over a year ago but did not have money to attend university. Although he was full of ambitions, he could not continue his studies, which for him was the only way he could improve his life. Ben was not so convinced because he had not gone to university and this did not prevent him from becoming wealthy. But Ben kept his thoughts to himself.

Kweku explained that he had planned to work in the mines for a year to save enough money to attend university. But after working for a year, he had not managed to save any money. He decided to work for another year to save the required amount. By the time Ben met him, he was two months into his second year of work. The young man was determined to save enough that year to resume his studies.

Since he started working in the mines, he had supported his entire family. He helped his younger siblings, who attended secondary school. He was responsible for paying for their tuition fees as well as their school uniforms and books.

Ben was invited to share a room with Kweku and his younger brother. The whole family quickly accepted him without anyone knowing anything about him. The next day, As Kweku was going to work in the mines, Ben followed him and started working in the mines. His time in the mines was an opportunity to understand the miners and local people better.

Each person's earnings depended on his ability to work harder, not smarter. It was all about physical strength. People worked the whole day with barely a rest but returned home with less than £1. This was their daily wages.

At night, Kweku would tell Ben how he wanted to study to become an engineer so that he could stop working as a miner. His dream after graduating did not involve owning a mining business or building machines to extract gold, but rather to serve those who already owned gold mining firms. He just wanted a decent office job so that he could earn enough to send his children to school. This was the ambition of most workers in the mining industry and across the country.

Every young person wanted to study if possible, to secure a job in the public administration or private firms. Foreigners owned most private businesses and the most affluent parts of the city. They fixed the prices of cocoa and coffee and bought them from local producers, who spent their days working hard to produce crops. Farmers had no choice but to agree on the prices, since they had no other means of selling their produce or transforming them.

The scenario was the same with gold and other precious stones. The buyers fixed the prices. Some locals managed to transform gold but on a very limited scale. Locally, few people were interested in buying gold, as most people did not have the means to make such purchases. Most individuals who had not been to university were unemployed. About 80 percent of graduates did not have a job either. Worst, even those who studied engineering were also job seekers, with only a handful of them trying to set up firms in their respective field. Teaching, being a bank clerk, or working in customer services were the career of choice for most people who had completed a master's degree. Those with a PhD were university lecturers, or working in more desirable positions, with only a few devoted to research and innovation.

The government had no budget for research and innovation, and private firms were not interested in investing in such areas. In fact, private companies that could support research were owned by westerners who brought solutions from their respective countries. Becoming a university lecturer was every young person's dream. It is where Kweku also wanted to be in 10 years if a private firm did not recruit him after his degree. He was planning to complete his PhD at the age of 29, however, before University, he wanted to spend another year in the mining industry digging gold to gather his tuition fee.

Ben spent one full month working in the mines and managed to save about £20. Before leaving he added £1,000 to the £20, he earned in the mining field, and it gave to Kweku as his parting gift. £1000 was a lot of money, more than what Kweku's parents had ever handled in a single year since they were born. This amount was worth millions in the current local currency and more than what Kweku needed for the whole duration of his studies. No one in Kweku's family had ever dreamed this possible, but by a heavenly fortune, Kweku had become a millionaire in one day. Kweku promised to leave the mines with immediate effect and to start preparing for his university debuts. He pledged to settle his tuition fee straight away to reserve his place for the next academic year. It was like a miracle, and a dream come true.

Ben was happy to have helped Kweku kick start his life's ambition. He left Ghana promising to keep in touch and to visit the following year. After Ben had left, he sent another £1,000 to Kweku to ensure that Kweku did not lack during his academic year. With over £2,000, Ben was convinced that Kweku would have a good start at university.

After Ghana, Ben continued to Senegal where he was hosted by Diop, whom he had met on the street. Diop's story was like Kweku's. He was a street seller and wanted to make enough money to return to his studies. Diop felt the government was not helpful. He believed that those in power only cared about themselves and their families, leaving common citizens without any support.

Ben helped Diop with his work for few days to understand his trade. After a week, Ben used his own money to start buying things to sell on the street like Diop. As he walked along the streets, he identified what was most in demand and focused on buying and selling those items. Ben only spent what he needed to survive and used his profit to buy more things to increase his capital. By the time he left Senegal, he had a capital of over £500 and over £300 in cash he had saved. In addition to the capital of around £500, he added £700 to the £300 he saved as profit and handed it all to Diop to help him fulfil his ambition. He was convinced that Diop could do well in his business. However, Diop only considered his business as a temporary occupation, as he wanted to return to his studies as soon as he had enough money. The £1000 plus the capital of £500 that Ben left was more than sufficient for Diop to enrol at University and continue selling on the weekends. In fact, this was a good capital to venture into a profitable business in Senegal. Immediately after Ben's departure, Diop got married and shelved his plan to further his education. He used the almost £1000 that Ben gave him, and part of his savings to organise his wedding. As a married man, he now had the responsibility of looking after his wife, his own family, and his in-laws. Within a year, Diop became a father and continued selling on the street. His capital was shrinking more and more with the demands placed on him. After three years of marriage and with two children, Diop was bankrupt. He found a job as a security officer with a salary of £40 a month.

Meanwhile, hoping that he had changed two people's lives, Ben continued his trip to Burkina Faso, Ivory Coast, Mali, Togo, Chad, Niger, Nigeria, Congo, and Cameroon. The stories were similar: people always complained about the lack of money and opportunities. In Nigeria and Cameroon for example, people complained about government corruption. Each young person was full of aspiration and ambitions; however, they were thwarted by a lack of funding. Before leaving each country, he visited, Ben offered financial support to his hosts.

By the time he returned home, Ben had spent over £100,000 helping people across the continent to fulfil their dreams. It was a rewarding trip for him to have had the chance to help. He was convinced that everyone he helped would change for the better. After all, everyone, everywhere Ben went, just wanted some financial support to kick-start their ambitions. Each person Ben met claimed that there were no opportunities in the land. For them, their poverty was due to lack of possibilities in their countries. They all believed that their struggle was due to lack of initial financial support to get them off the ground. Ben, despite being a self- made billionaire, would have ended up believing in this widespread assumption if he did not know first-hand that each can forge for themselves the type of life they desire. He had no doubt, nonetheless that, at least 90% of people he supported would rise above poverty and change their family's history.

When Ben visited Congo, for example, he realised that people only focused on appearances.

Each young person's ambition was to have enough money to go into music or to dress better than others and those who studied wanted to run the country. In the Central African Republic, everyone who was educated up to A level standard aspired to become a politician. Nevertheless, he still supported his hosts' ambitions. Throughout his trip, every young person he met was unsatisfied with their respective governments. They were full of dreams, either to study or to become politicians. Only a few of people dreamed of having their own business, and only a few of them knew what they wanted in life and were determined live to their dreams. The majority only had wishful thoughts about their future, with no real action to materialise their dreams. As we all know, Wishful thinking is the formation of beliefs and making decisions according to what might be pleasing to imagine instead of by appealing to evidence, rationality, or reality. It is a product of resolving conflicts between belief and desire.

Everyone's hopes, and dreams were on the government or God to change their live. Even amongst those who knew what they wanted; many changed their plans as soon as they had a bit of money. For example, Kweku, Ben' first host, never went to the university. After Ben's departure from Accra, Kweku changed his plan.

In all countries visited, Ben, saw opportunities for small businesses, or agriculture, for mining, for farming, for tourism and even for industrial revolution.

By the end of his trip, he had identified a common trait amongst Africans: Their mindset. People were more interested in what they could have immediately, what they could get from others or what they could do to improve other people's lives. Few people cared about the future.

Everyone was prone to conning others and ready to engage in corruption. Everyone saw the state as a distribution centre and hoped to receive from the state. Those who had a job in the state administrative system saw themselves as owners and rulers, and the state's wealth became their possession and a gift they grasped and squander. For example, people unscrupulously embezzled public funds or public properties. Many also believed government jobs were ideal, as they didn't require any hard work. Also, people earned more than their annual income from bribery. The spirit of ethnic discrimination was the norm. Only those who knew someone secured a job, even in the private sector. Every position was filled through recommendations and introductions.

Each person with a responsibility to hire staff had their agents, who introduced candidates that paid the right price for the job. People preferred to give preferential treatment to those who came from their ethnicity, or those who paid a high bribe price, irrespective of whether they had the right skillset. Few people thought about the necessity of moving the country forward. Innovation was just limited to copying what others were already doing. People engaged in the same types of businesses they had seen their neighbours start and sold the same goods or services.

Original ideas were scant, and once there was one, everyone copied the idea, but badly, without any improvement.

Throughout his African tour, Ben identified, people, wanting quick wins. Their focus was on the present with no consideration at all for the future. They wasted no time planning the future or thinking seriously about the profound effects of their actions on their land. For most of them, life was limited to the five senses.

People talked about the future, but their actions were geared toward fulfilling their immediate needs. No one wanted to delay their gratification. No one wanted to make sacrifices for a better tomorrow. When there was something to gain from any situation or circumstances, no one hesitated to seize the opportunity, no matter what the consequences. Everyone hated poverty but had no plan to overcome it. All Africans thought that it was someone else's responsibility to eliminate poverty in their land. Ambitions were very limited the present personal gain. Ben rarely met anyone who wanted to become a world-renowned individual in their field. The only exception was for footballers, as they could not make ends meet in their local teams or countries.

Ben was shocked by people's attitude and pondered about what makes great nations great. He concluded that greatness could not be conceived elsewhere than in the mind. Without a serious ambition, imagination, or a dream to become great, one is unlikely to become great.

The idea of greatness also depends on what one perceives to be great. According to the people Ben met, great people were those who were able to eat three meals a day. Impacting the world was not their ambition. None of them ever tried to find the secret of building a car, a train, a TV set, or radio. For them, these things were made by others, and had become trivial things. The most they could do was to learn how to repair or mend them when they broke down.

Most people saw themselves as poor and were convinced that they were unable to change their situation, at least without someone lese help and when help came, they quickly abandoned their ambition and squandered the money in a matter of days. The popular belief was studying at university will provide jobs and then money, however, the education system was itself a total let down, as it only trained people to become servants, with heads full, rather than tailoring their programmes to their country's needs.

Education was a linear process, which went from primary to secondary education, from there to university, and then to a job if there was one available. Everyone wanted to be offered a job rather than trying to create one. Each wanted the government to create employment for them. No one saw in themselves a future employer, even though they were potentially a great businessman like Ben.

Throughout his groups of companies, Ben employed over 20,000 people directly. The number was much larger, and potentially triple, if we include those who benefited from his supply chain and those whose employment depended on his businesses.

After his visit, Ben regularly sent money to support his friends across Africa and other parts of the continent. Apparently, none of them knew exactly who he was. Had they known, they would have expected even more from him, even though he didn't owe them anything.

Two years after his first visit to Accra, Ben returned to visit Kweku. To his great surprise, Kweku was still living in the same house, with his parents, still working in the gold mines and was now married with a child. Despite Ben's support, Kweku had not changed much. He had managed to buy a plot of land next to his parents' slum where he wanted to erect a home and move in with his wife and child. During Ben's second stay, Kweku gave him thousands of reasons why he stopped pursuing his ambition. He said that after Ben's departure, his parents became ill and he had to use the money to save their lives. With the regular support Ben sent to Kweku said that he used the money to support his wife, child and brothers. Obviously, the situation could only go from bad to worse, since he was still planning on having more children, with no plan for their upkeep. After his investigations, Ben found out that Kweku used the money received from Ben to organise his wedding. People said that it was one of the greatest weddings they had ever seen in the area. So, Kweku sacrificed his future for the sake of pleasure. In the beginning, Kweku pointed to lack of capital and financial support to pursue his ambitions. With more than what he needed, he remained poor. **Why? Because his problem was never the lack of financial assistance. He had the wrong mindset and would never change or move above the confinements of destitution with the same mindset.**

To Ben, he painted an endless catalogue of the bad things that had happened to him after departure from Ghana, as if bad things only waited for money to start manifesting. This was a common belief in this part of the world anyway. Some of the things he said were pure inventions to justify his bad judgement, his failure to attract sympathy.

Diop's story was similar; in fact, apart from one person, everyone Ben had helped remained the same or worse after he had helped them. The only person that had progressed was a young man from Cameroon, who was focused and knew exactly what he wanted. His ambition was to open a garage and to have the best one in his town. With Ben's help, he quickly started his garage business. In less than two years, he had the best garage in Kumba. People had begun to call him a witch, as they could not believe how he could make such progress in such a short amount of time. If he lost anyone in his family, he was accused of selling them in secret sects to make money. This was a widespread belief across Africa. Some people went as far as thinking that to overcome poverty, human sacrifice was needed through witchcraft, to attract good luck or money. So, those who made it were believed to be witches or sorcerers if they didn't' belong to a sect.

With the help and support provided to people here, and thereby both the international community and people of goodwill like Ben, only a handful of Africans improve their situation. Most of them remain poor, despite their first wish for a small push to help them kick start in life. After a little boost, people ask for another push, and another push and the revolving doors continues with no real improvements. It had become evident, even to Ben, that aid and financial support is not really what is required to overcome poverty in Africa.

What is necessary is a change of mindset. A total transformation of attitudes. Any change that does not start from the mind has less impact and it's hard to change a man who doesn't want to change. It is easy to bring someone to the water, but he will have to drink the water by himself. Even in the poorest countries on earth, there are billionaires. Therefore, poverty is in the mind, and ordinary citizens have common minds, and common minds live common lives. Poverty comes from a lack of the right mental attitude or mental capacity to choose the right path in life. Poverty is a decision. A poor man has a poor mind. No land is so poor that it cannot provide for its inhabitants and what one gets depends on the demand pressed upon the land. A good result is based upon the right mindset and the curiosity to look beyond the appearances for opportunities. There are always possibilities for those who can use their minds and apply it right.

Poor people want a comfortable ride. Their ambition is limited if not lacking and their efforts are dispersed, and their plans vanish once they can afford a good meal. This can only be the choice of fools, short-sighted individuals whose minds and vision are limited. They look around and see no opportunities. They see themselves as worthless and poor, and poor they remain. Those who dream big are young Africans but when they have a job, they become like their fathers and start doing what they use to criticise, and half of a century of the same type of education system had changed nothing in the continent. Innovations and technologies and foreign concepts are imported. What is thought in Africa brings no solutions to their problems.

Any individual who cannot fend for himself is dependent upon someone, as such, he is either a slave or a servant. Any man who cannot protect himself is vulnerable to attacks and a potential loser in the battlefield. Furthermore, any person who cannot replenish his supplies is susceptible to starvation. A man with an empty stomach has no dignity. Even in the Bible, poverty caused people to eat their children. People became victim to all sorts of abuses and obliged to do things that they wouldn't normally do if they had something to eat.

It can be observed that poor people eat their crops along with the seeds and offer themselves for a guarantee to survive when there is no choice- they become the shield- the reason why they receive the bullets. No one's situation is in the hand of another unless he chooses to make it that way. Each human decides what he makes of his life, no matter where he lives.

Whether you are rich or poor, you can do something about your situation, unless you have a mental disability. **Poverty is a choice, not a gift. It is a choice, not a fate. You can change your fate in no time.** Some people's ambitions cannot be fulfilled at a local level, and the road is opened to whoever wants to advance. Border barriers are only artificial. He who is willing can overcome every human-made obstacle. He who knows what he wants and will get it exactly when the time is right. It is up to each to claim their place and stand their ground. The solution is around the corner. If you are willing to take the time required, if you persist with a clear plan, and if you know what is it that you are looking, you will find it.

Continue to search with faith in your ability to find a solution from within. Poverty is not your nature but only your mindset can settle the matter and make. You are a success, a spirit that can do all things.

Chapter 14

The Real Source of Wealth: Everyone's Got It!

Is wealth in the land or the minds? In other words, what determines people's wealth? is it their mindset or their land? Is The answer to this question is essential for one who wants to understand why some people are poor and others wealthy? Why do we find wealthy people in the desert and some of the most impoverished individuals in the middle of rich and diverse vegetation? Generally, many people believe if you have a land full of natural resources, it will create wealth for it citizens- therefore, there is no justification for people to be poor in such environment. Let us test this theory: The global GDP will be around $85.9 trillion in 2018. Africa, with an estimated population of approximately 1.3 billion people living in 54 different countries. Africa Despite being considered as a resource-rich continent its GDP is only $2.19 trillion growing at 3.7% per year, compared to Apple which is the bigger or richest company in the world with an estimated net worth of $1.3 Trillion, Microsoft net worth is estimated at $1 trillion, Facebook $74 billion, Amazon $115.6 billion. We can see that four companies' income is bigger than the income of a whole continent estimated to be the richest in resources.

These companies are not based in the resources rich continent and these companies are people's technologies and creative companies. They have no natural resources on their own and are the fruit of individual thoughts. This assessment implies that the wealth creation resides in the mind and not in the land. Contrary to this popular belief, we see that despite African's natural resources, the continent is languishing in poverty and hunger and the trend continues every year.

The raw material used in cosmetics, pharmaceuticals, jewellery, manufacturing, and technology industries across the world are extracted from Africa but the process of inventing those tool s and products are not African. In clear, people discovered African resources and found the way to add value to them. This process of discovering and value adding is a though process and resides in the mind, not in the land. It is therefore not surprising, however controversial, and ironic, though true, to note that, despite its significant natural heritage, African countries remain poor, when developed countries' industries cannot survive without Africa's resources. This observation makes one wonder and suggests that what makes a country rich or poor is how its citizens think.

How do we then define a poor or underdeveloped country? Is it a country with no natural resources or a country with lofty-minded citizens? What make countries like Belgium, Switzerland, the United Kingdom or Luxemburg wealthy nations? Do they necessarily have desirable natural resources? Which European country is as rich and diverse like DR Congo in natural resources? Where else do we find the type of diversity that is available in Cameroon? Which African country lacks natural resources? How come all African countries remain below the poverty level, despite their natural wealth?

More astonishingly, why do we have billionaires in some of the poorest countries in the world and some of the poorest people in wealthy nations? Does a country necessarily need to be endowed with immense natural resources to become rich? Why does Congo, so rich in minerals and natural resources, have some of the poorest citizens?

Niger, Mali, Chad, and Burkina Faso are considered amongst some of the poorest countries in the world because they have fewer natural resources, with mostly dried lands, which limit their agricultural potential and production. These countries are also counted amongst the poorest nations on earth. Nevertheless, we have millionaires and billionaires in these countries. People have different views about how these people accumulated their wealth; nonetheless, they are still millionaires and billionaires and better off. Some people say that these countries' current millionaires have benefited from the advantage of being the first in their field of business. But we can also argue that they lived in the same country, and at the same time, as those who are poor, but they managed to rise above the crowd. Their ability to distinguish themselves from the crowd must be due how they think. They must have had or done something that the poor did not do.

For those who claim that the government helped some of the richest people and so on, I would say that these individual, if they have been helped, they most have done something to put them in the position of being supported. Even with help, not everyone succeeds.

We know this from Ben's experience from his African expedition. Receiving support does not necessarily guarantee success. To be successful, one needs a healthy, smart, and astute mindset. So, no matter who helped a billionaire, or where they first got theirs to start with, their success is due to their mental attitude. Successful people have a certain mindset.

Millionaires and successful people are those who may be doing the same things that everyone does, but differently. They think in a certain way and behave in a certain way. They are willing to succeed, and success is their obsession. They fail by chance. They succeed because they want to achieve and have charted their way through their success.

Millionaires are those who are never satisfied with their current position. They see opportunities where others do not. They understand peoples' needs where there are apparently no needs. They create opportunities and invent new things that become required, and by so doing, they attract income through their services and goods that meet other people's needs. They do not necessarily follow what others do, and certainly, they do not do what poor people do. They create a roadmap for their success through their thought processes. Simply put, they are smart! They are witty and wise.

Wisdom means doing the right thing all the time or doing the right things most of the times. Therefore, smart people are those who use their mind well most of the time. They translate their thoughts into solutions that meet people's needs, and people pay for those solutions.

A solution-bringer will always attract reward from a solution-seeker. A solution-seeker pays the price tag for a solution they receive. Solution-bringers will sail through life better than solutions-users. People pay a higher price for a service, innovation, and for a product because someone has used his imagination to add value to them.

At a raw state, in their natural state, commodities are very cheap. Only innovative people increase the value to what already exists. Suppose that people are richer because they live in a more fertile land, the question will be: Why do some people living in wealthy nations poor, and why would some people choose to live in the poor land? Each group most have made a choice, based on their perception of the world.

Most people who live in grass fields and savannahs came from the coastal lands. They found it too difficult to subdue the sea. They found it easier to live in the mountains than planes. There is tale according to which, some people left the coast because they were afraid that a giant would come from the sea and swallow them. Another story, from a different culture, says that their people were the first inhabitants of the coast, but they left because they believed that one day the sea level would rise and flood their village, killing the inhabitants.

Some people choose the desert as their preferred home. They are happy in the wilderness. People live all over the earth, sometimes in the weirdest and remotest places, by choice. Many people live in deserts all over the world, including the Alaskan desert. Whether in the wilderness or on the coast, whether in a fertile land full of minerals and natural resources or in areas deprived of precious resources, there are wealthy and poor people.

Russia is one of the richest countries in the world in natural resources, but its economy is not the richest. While the country boasts extensive natural resources, the Russian population is not the most affluent. The standard of living in Russia is lower than the standard of life in central Europe. Most of the Russian population is in fact poor. In contrast, Japan is the fourth richest nation on earth, but they don't have the same natural resources as Russia. The UK is the fifth largest economy in the world, yet, the UK subsoil is less endowed with natural resources than the Democratic Republic of Congo's. The USA is the first world power but was only formed as a country on July 4, 1776; however, the basis for its greatness was conceived from its inception. A thought process that made the USA great and richer. The USA's foundation was based on a mindset. This mindset. The fore founders of the USA wanted to make their country the greatest, and it is surely the greatest country on earth. They set trends for innovation, inventions, and business excellence. Before its discovery, the USA was always there, and its natural resources were always present. The USA was not an empty land, although it was desolate and almost uninhabited in most parts because indigenous people did not occupy the whole land. However, it was always potentially the richest country at the time, controversially, those who lived there were poor. People who discovered the USA saw in it the land of opportunities and wealth. They did not only make it the most desirable place in the world to live; they made it a great country.

Like the USA, the colonial powers saw Africa as a new paradise. They identified various resources in Africa that they used to power their industries and change their people's lives. They used most of the African resources to build their nations and enriched their respective countries. Residents felt unhappy and proclaimed their independences. Since becoming independent over 60 years ago, they have not made any real advances, and most of their population live below the poverty level, despite having the most fertile lands and rich subsoils. Henceforth, despite knowing the richness of their land, Africans have not made efforts to transform their natural resources and commodities by themselves. Their lack of creativity and like-mindedness makes it impossible for them to meet their own needs. They see industrial advances as someone else's duty. Most African nations don't know what they need and want, therefore, they cannot meet their own needs, their populations' or the worlds'. Those who make discoveries in their land become their masters, with the power to set prices for their local and national commodities and resources.

Africans' dependency makes them vulnerable. Most of their natural resources are transformed elsewhere and resold to them ten thousand times the price of the raw material. Poor Africans now use all their income to pay for imported products and services, thus taking their money out of their system. Africans could have been better off if they were able to create desirable products and services.

Like Africa, indigenous people who lived in America were gatherers, not planners. Eaters, not thinkers. Gatherers gather and empty the land, whereas thinkers develop solutions to improve and enrich, multiply and replenish the land Australia, for example, was populated with prisoners, and the country was not formally founded until 1891, although people lived there. Australia was established long after Africa had been visited and explored by the West. Cameroon, for example, signed some treaties signed at the beginning of the 19th century, and instead of copying from the West what was desirable, they signed agreements for the West to protect them. Which type of protection did they want? Those who were seeking shelter had never answered this question, and it's hard for us to answer on their behalf. We can only conclude that they had a limited view of the world, and brought upon themselves the calamity of domination, imperialism, and colonialism of which they are now the victims. The colonisers were bright people. They were well-organised, and saw themselves as great people, and indeed knew what they wanted. Only those who know what they want to get the best and only those who think great make significant progress.

Administrators who were sent by Britain to run Australia were planning ways to improve their lives in the country. For example, they began using prisoners to build roads. They realised that prisoners could be used to develop Australia instead of wasting their time in prison, and they used them well. Coming from behind, Australia is now considered one of the richest nations on earth, whereas almost all African people still live in destitution despite their past exploits thousands of years ago. Their poverty is due to their lack of self-confidence, which creates a self-limiting mindset. They live in constant fear of poverty; therefore, one will quickly steal from his employer once he is given the opportunity. By stealing they hope to make as much money as possible in a short time so that, whatever happens, they will be protected. They ignore that in making their employer weaker, they become miserable together. Had they innovated and brought creativity to improve the services within the organisation where they worked, everyone would have been better off. With their small-minded mentality, they will continue to be impoverished, if they keep embezzling, or using imported solutions for their problems and needs.

When travelling across Africa, we see comfortable houses with roofs that protect people better. People are now sleeping in more comfortable beds. Medical progress is offering people the chance to live longer, and new drugs are relieving people from pain. People can now reach the USA on the same day by air, travelling 8000 miles in less than 12 hours. It would have taken months to cover this distance 100 years ago. People now instantly speak and see each other at the same time from different countries aid by technology. This was not possible 20 years ago. Many discoveries are being made which help people around the world; these developments show man's ability. Wealth and knowledge are increasing in the world. It is evident that the increase of wealth is due to knowledge increase. At the same time, the number of people living on the planet is growing and, unexpectedly, the number of poor people is also increasing. One would have assumed that with wealth increase, poverty would be on the decrease. It is not the case. This is because the world is faster than before and the slower to think will remain behind, thus poor. Still, at the same time, people nowadays have even more opportunities to make money- and come out of poverty- than before, if they so wish.

The increased wealth in the world is due to people's ability to think creatively. This means that wealth creation is linked to a mindset. Wealth depends upon each person's ability to use his mind.

One of the great inventors could have been you, but instead of finding your way to your purpose, you spend your days looking for food. This is why you are still poor, because without solving problems for others you will never gather enough resources to meet your own needs.

Those who have more wealth and more privileges are those who solve other people's problems. For example, great inventors have made a fortune. Bill Gates, Steve Jobs and Larry Paige have created solutions that people desire across the world, and by bringing solutions to people's needs, they have created a fortune for themselves. Their innovation is a result of their thought processes.

Nations where significant discoveries have been made are better off than countries that possess the most natural resources. The USA is a wealthy country, and this wealth derives from their ability to discover new ways of doing things; their ability to create and to invent solutions they sell to the world.

Just to show the importance of creative thoughts, it has been estimated that services account for about 80% of the UK's revenue. This means that people make more money from services in the UK than from products. In other words, British people are astute in the way they sell their ideas. As previously mentioned, these, ideas help them remain one of the five richest countries in the world.

People are encouraged to develop their mindset, to devise solutions to problems. Solutions to problems bring wealth and freedom. The more people are free to think, the less likely they are to live in poverty. Individuals who don't think cannot innovate. Animals cannot innovate. Animals spend their days and night fighting for food and survival; their lives are about survival. Those who think day and night about what to eat are not far from animals. Those who only think regarding survival will never experience freedom, wealth, and happiness. Over-focusing on the needs of the tummy distracts people from thinking deeply, creatively, and innovatively.

Each land is as rich as its population's ability to think. America before discovery was always a rich land, but nothing else was happening there.

It was a rich land inhabited by people with poor minds. The change that took place in the USA was more of a mental attitude than the condition of the land. In some cases, new settlers had to bring water from far to make life possible in remote areas. A government system was designed to ensure a stable society with a sense of national identity. Most of their citizenship programmes focus on making their citizens believe that they are the best.

So, what shall we continue to say about the wealth of a nation? Is it created by the land or by people? I guess the answer is that people create wealth. A man can transform his environment and make new discoveries, whereas animals are still eating their prey in a raw state. Humans' extraordinary progress is attributed to their ability to think. Again, we go back to people's conditions, regarding wealth and poverty. If people create wealth, and if there is a link between the way people think, and the way they live, it can be concluded that the better one's thoughts, the deeper one's thoughts, the better the solutions they bring to problem-solving. The better the solution, the greater the income their solution generates, and the better their living conditions.

If you think more creatively, you will find solutions that will set you free from lack and ignorance. If quality thinking creates quality solutions, and if quality solutions create wealth, it is possible to conclude that Africa lacks quality thinkers! People talk about the inefficiency of the government and corruption. People should take personal responsibility for their actions. If each is failing to do what they are supposed to do, if they are not thinking right, it suggests that they are not quality thinkers, and this confirms our theory.

We have already seen how African politicians are only interested in themselves. However, those politicians are elected by university lecturers and students who sell their votes for instant gratification. They sell their future in exchange for bread. During electoral campaigns, most Africans sell their votes for immediate income. So why complain about the quality of government they have put in place? Why complain about the government when each person who attains any position of power stops thinking and starts eating instead? They use what they find without any plan for multiplying or replenishing it. No wonder there is no continuity. Each African is guilty. Guilty are those who help create these conditions through their actions and those maintain those conditions. Every poor person must accept some degree of responsibilities; either they are helping to create the conditions of poverty, or they are helping perpetuate it. Those who do not want to be poor can find their way out. They can think their way out.

Let us look at Democratic Republic of Congo, one of the richest countries in the world in natural resources. Congo, despite its natural resources, is one of the poorest countries because of people's standard of living. Why is it so? They focus on their natural resources rather than creating a system that will guarantee a better future for all.

Better systems create conditions for people to thrive. The creation of the right governance and administrative systems requires the right mindset, where each stakeholder makes a sacrifice instead of focussing on their vain ambitions. If this attitude doesn't stop, the country will always be poor, despite having sought-after natural resources. It is not enough to have resources. What do you do with resources you don't know their utility?

Everything man needs to excel is already available to him, no matter where he is. You need to understand that value of anything before you can add value to it. Knowing what to do with something requires experimentation, a level of thinking. To improve your social conditions, you must first develop hypotheses, projects, and plans, and then test and confirm them. Therefore, the wealth is in the mind, not in the land. The land may be a means to wealth creation, but the mind remains an agent for transformation. The mind is the instrument through which man will make sense of the world around him. Man uses his mind to identify what is useful. He needs to use his mind to determine what to do, and then use his body to make tools that transform his mental experience into material things.

Countries can experience a change in a short time, once they have changed their mindset. Congo can change, Cameroon can change, Burkina Faso can change, South Sudan can change. Lasting solutions to African problems should focus on mind transformation first, before transforming the physical landscape of the continent. The weight given to mind-changing programmes will accelerate the speed with which people can create wealth for the continent. Education systems should focus on creating minds that are free to think. It should encourage students to believe in their abilities and to have confidence in their potential to make an impact on the world. The more the focus is on mind transformation, the better people will identify, at their level, what is required to make their contribution worthwhile.

My philosophy is about man's ability to fulfil his purpose, and my focus is on better living. I am convinced that no man is free and happy in poverty. To be happy, man needs to meet his spiritual, social, and physiological needs. He cannot achieve this without the ability to think and plan.

Africa's population is growing and has reached one billion people. It is, therefore, necessary to plan how their people's needs will be met in the future and put in place systems to help them think creatively so they may thrive. There is no land so poor that they have nothing to offer. Even the desert offers the sand. However, there are poor minds everywhere, people who refuse to think-those individuals with poor mindsets.

Chapter 15

If You Don't Ask, You Don't Get

Ben had visited almost all African countries. It was now time to go beyond the continent. On his first trip to Europe, Ben stopped at a fast-food restaurant. He had always heard about fast food restaurants, and he wanted to taste their food.

As Ben entered a McDonald's restaurant, he sat on the first empty chair he saw and waited and waited for over 30 minutes. As he was waiting, people who arrived after him were being served while he was apparently being ignored. Some of the clients directly typed at machine terminal inside the restaurant and would be served. As Ben waited, he became frustrated when he realised that people who came after him were being served, while no one took notice of him. He could see workers bringing orders back and forth. Some workers passed by him without saying a word. He continued to sit and wait, but no one attended to him as workers continued to move around the restaurant serving everyone except him.

Just as he wanted to leave, he proceeded to the counter to have a word with the manager. He wanted to understand why he had been ignored for nearly an hour. As soon as he approached the counter, an employee addressed him graciously, with perfect smile and courtesy:

"Welcome to our restaurant sir, have you been here before"?

Ben replied "no".

The employee continued, "we are one of the best fast-food chains in the world and have a whole raft of menus. We have menus for vegans, vegetarians, ethnics, and can cater for everyone. Is there any food that you do not eat sir? Do you eat meat? Do you want me to recommend our best menu for you?" the employee was comprehensive, professional and helpful.

Ben was lost for words, but before placing his order, he asked: "Why didn't anyone come to me when I sat there for nearly an hour?"

The employee apologised and explained that no one noticed that he was sitting and waiting to be served. He explained that if they had known, someone would have come to him, moreover; "here you ask for what you want at the counter or order from the computer terminal and your order will be ready for you. So, everyone has to proceed to the counter to be served or order at the machine".

The lesson was clear. If you do not ask, you do not get, and you get what you ask for. This was Ben's exact philosophy. If you do not place a demand, you get nothing. Ben was at the right place, at the right time, waiting for what he wanted, and what he wanted was within his reach. However, he could not get it, because he hadn't asked for it.

The world is also like that. God created man with the power to rule over the earth and every living thing. Everything man needs is available, but he needs to go and get it. Each needs to claim what they need. The first step for getting what you need is to know exactly what is it that you want. Ben was served because he articulated what he wanted.

Ben would have left the restaurant, hungry and frustrated, without being served if he had not asked. Furthermore, he could have continued the same mistake repeatedly, if he didn't try to find out why he was being ignored. Being at the right place, at the right time is not enough. It is not sufficient to be where opportunities abound, nor is it enough to know what you want; you need to make a demand. It is probably why Africans can be impoverished while living in a wealthy continent.

No one was created to be underprivileged, and no one should be lowly, but few people know their rights. Even if they did, they do not exercise those rights. Poor people do not take their time to find out the correct way to get want they want. For example, suppose you have inherited a property in London. The deed and the keys to the property are posted to you in Birmingham, where you are homeless. You will remain homeless if you are still in Birmingham. Until you reach London, you will not occupy your property, and your situation may not change. This shows how many homeowners or potential homeowners remain homeless.

Each human being is the owner of all his desires. There is no limit as to what man can ask for and receive; however, he can only achieve what he needs by taking the right steps. Some people are too full of themselves to dare, while others are too concerned about what others may say about them if they fail. So, individual behaviour needs to be adapted according to circumstances, environment, and context. Farming in the desert requires different techniques compared to farming in swamps. This is the way life is. Those who lack, should not be lacking, if they apply their knowledge correctly. They need to use the power within, to find the right solution, based on their environment.

It follows that each person gets what he wants if he places the right request at the right place. Ben would have been served straight away if upon entering the restaurant, he had enquired about the method of placing an order. Had he asked that question, he would not have waited for over an hour. This common sense is not a familiar place with poor people. They assume that things should always be the way they think they should be anywhere and at any time. They presume that someone else will always meet their needs, and when their needs are not fulfilled, they complain about the world being unfair. They do the same thing everywhere, and at all seasons, and expect the best and see injustices everywhere. They see success and someone ability to have three meals a day.

So, what is a success and how do you achieve it? Why do we need to succeed? To answer these questions, we may ask ourselves if we can talk about successful lions, monkeys, pigs or goats. Are there successful chickens or donkeys? If the answer is no, then the conclusion may be that success is a prerogative of human beings. The privilege of men and women. This goes back to the beginning: Every man has the potential to succeed. He is naturally and latently successful. But he can only become societally and visibly successful if he uses his invisible power of thoughts to make things happen.

Hegel asserted that the reason governs the world, thus highlighting the importance of thought processes in the transformation of the world. This coined with Descartes' idea of humans as thinking beings, emphasising that success is limited to humans, amidst countless species of animals in the world, some of which are very intelligent. Human's achievements thus come down to their ability to think and to imagine.

A man is a spirit, and by tapping into the world of the spirit, he can identify, understand, and conceive things that should be, but are not yet materially visible. Subsequently, to become successful, one must see beyond the now through his spiritual eyes.

We can imagine things, and we can see things, even with our eyes closed. We can imagine a thing or a situation, and we can make it occur if we so wish to. It is possible to imagine the steps that can help us achieve a dream. Although this may not be immediately possible, nonetheless, the more we believe and try, the closer we get to the solution by eliminating unrealistic hypotheses, until we grasp a real or immutable solution; the truth of the matter, the ultimate solution. Now, it appears easy in theory, but it is also easy in practice, if you think about it. People believe that life is not easy because of the price they must pay to reach the solution they need. Being successful requires commitment, hard work and sacrifice.

Ben asked the right question and got the right answer at McDonald's. The right answer enabled him to take the next step.

Sometimes, we do all the right things and fail to take the final step. You may get the keys and the deeds to your inherited house in London and make the journey to London, but once in front of the house, if you do not unlock the door, you will not get in. As long as you stay at the front door, you will still be homeless.

You need, therefore, to claim your due, and pay the required price. You may require financial support to reach your goal, and you may not receive any financial support when you need, however, applying the right thinking will help you to identify how you can obtain the finances that you need.

In your journey, you may need other people who can make a living from your situation, but whom, nonetheless, will help you make your own living. By being useful to yourself, you become valuable to others. This means playing your part in the world rendezvous of giving and receiving. To get other people on board, or to stay on board yourself, you need to be and remain focused. Despite the hurdles, you must believe that you can and will succeed.

Ben's story is evidence of the principle of power and success that is latent in every human being. Through conscious efforts and intelligent use of one's mind each, each can develop his mental faculties, and grow in whatever direction he chooses. There are no limits as to how poor a man can be. His level of poverty will depend on him. Similarly, his ability to achieve great things and his level of success are also in his hands.

No man is yet to become so great that no one else could match his worth. The comparison may reside in their difference, unlike what they have achieved. He who has embraced and pursued his dream will forever be known to many earthly residents. The limitless possibilities are inherent to human nature. However, only those who can stand their ground with a sound awareness of their worth can reach their goals.

Great people are always greater than their ideas and their deeds. They are linked to the power that knows no limits. The Bible states that "Greater is he that is in you, than he that is in the world" (1 John 4:4). Within each person resides the power to become great and to excel. Poor people are those who cannot spare the required time to search for their purpose in life, by tapping into the great power that is in them.

He who stands his ground is he who knows a difference between himself, and the lowest animal. He who wastes no time searching who pushed them from behind, but dreams day and night on how to get ahead, will surely get to his destination. If you are looking for your mistakes or other people's mistakes, there will be enough to occupy a lifetime. There is no point spending your life searching for injustices and justifying why you are poor. The reasons you are poor now are known; the most important thing is how to get out of your present situation since observation alone will not bring you water to drink or add value to another person's life.

Only your actions will improve your conditions; moreover, your improved conditions will inevitably have a positive impact on others. Therefore, the power of conscious growth is in your hands. You alone can develop and increase your wealth and worth. A person who does not grow will regress, and no conscious human being will endure stagnation with pleasure.

He who has chosen this route with gladness is either mentally deficient, or ignorant of his nature, and he should not complain when at some point, he is not able to meet his own needs. He should also be prepared to understand why those who spared no efforts to advance are enjoying the pleasure of conscious growth.

There are no possibilities and abilities in any human being that are not in every individual. So, you are able, and you can achieve what others have been able to achieve. It is accepted that humans are equals. However, some people know how to improve their lives while others only complain about their situation. This is what makes a difference and creates inequalities. Though all men are given the same mandate at birth- to overcome, subdue, multiply and replenish the earth- only a handful of people fulfil this mandate.

We can overcome situations and circumstances, and our ability to overcome challenges, to subdue what our physical body, our ability to perceive the reality beyond our five senses, is crucial. Our belief in possibilities determines our position and wealth and our relentlessness to multiply and replenish our supply is a key factor in determining the number of reserves we have in store. The poor man's storehouse is empty, while the rich man's storehouse is full and will never run dry.

A rich man doesn't have any potential or abilities that cannot be found in a poor man. The difference between a poor man and a rich man resides in the way they both think. A rich man thinks of possibilities and has a fecund imagination. He gives pre-eminence to his spiritual faculties, whereas a poor man's efforts tend to converge towards meeting his physical urges. A poor man wants to eat, and a rich man wants to plant. A rich man aims at long-term solutions, but a poor man focuses on the here and now. A rich man is strategic, but a poor man is reactive. A poor man lives as he goes and when the supply runs out he is stark.

A rich man imagines the best outcomes and finds ways to get there. He is aware of his earthly mandate and knows that anything that can be imagined or perceived in detail is possible. Anything that man can think of is possible to accomplish.

In sand, a poor man sees only mud and dirt, while a rich mind sees blocks to erect

strong structures, to build roads, to make glasses for bottles, dishes, mirrors, glasses for doors and windows, ceramic to carry electric power- this is possible- etc. A poor man sees sand as useless, while a rich man can make all sorts of useful things, tools, and products from the same material.

In trees, a poor mind sees only the wood to cook his food, and possibly timbers to build a makeshift home. Conversely, a rich mind looks at the trees and sees polished furniture, slate for roofs, and paper. A rich man uses the same to make all sorts of objects with a price tag out of the poor minds' reach. A poor man may be the owners and grower of the trees, but he knows not its full potential, thus gets less for his produce.

Now that he knows the importance of his trees and sand, he still can't be bothered to learn the secret of adding value to them. What he wants is a penny in addition to his original price, and when this is done, he understands that satisfaction cannot come from his dependence on his resources in their raw or natural state. Value is added when a further transformation process takes place. What does the poor man do? He organises pity parties

POOR LAND OR POOR MINDS

and rallies other poor minds like himself to cry and chant over the rooftops about all the injustices in the world. He sees injustices everywhere, as if he had been made poor by anyone other than himself. Had he taken his time to look at his resources with an enquiring mind, he would have identified the best way to add value to attract the right price tag.

For a poor mind, the land is desolate if no animals can be found to hunt. A land is useless if the trees cannot produce their fruits straight away for food. What a poor man wants is to enjoy without efforts. He makes no investigations to understand the quality of the subsoil he lives on. Wise people know that the visible world is temporal and corruptible, and the real world is invisible. The invisible is permanent, while the visible is mutable. A poor mind lives with a short-term view of the world; he is concerned only with the present moment and does not give due consideration to the future. For the poor, the reality is all he can see, touch, a taste or feel and smell.

A poor mind is like a car, controlled from without, though having a power within. With external command, the engine cannot move. No matter how powerful it is, it idles, unless a

program has been fixed to the central command for this purpose. But when, at his will, his owner or a borrower presses the ignition, the power activates, and the car is ready for service. The car will only be used when the owner deems it necessary or starts the engine. **Poor people's hidden power can be activated in much the same manner as a cars. Despite having immense power dormant, poor people need to tap into it to change their lives wilfully.**

Those who change the world are those who use their imagination to create new services or goods that are appealing to many. Such men need no advertisement. They are always in demand. Their services improve the world, and consequently their living conditions. Such a person experiences no scarcity that cannot be compensated or acquired through exchange with the proceeds of his services. Such a man will be happier and will be motivated to offer more to get more. His efforts serve the whole human race.

Every person should claim their place as master of their circumstances. They should contribute their gifts to humanity. A successful man is fruitful and produces during all seasons.

This is again the reason why he is always in demand. A successful man perceives the end from the beginning and spends all his efforts finding his way to that end. When what he is reaching for is great and good for many, financial abundance will follow, for others will understand how they can meet their own needs through his offering.

There are undreamed, unthinkable and unlimited possibilities in ordinary individuals like Ben and I. The common man is a man who has resigned, and gives up on self, either because he thinks he is no longer able to do anything worth noticing, or by ignorance.

Ben was a common man at birth; so too is each great man is common at birth. However, no common man can become a great man. **A great man is a common man at birth who growing up understands his potential and realises that he is no longer common. An extraordinary man is simply the one who refuses to remain common. Every man is potentially a great man, but each man has the choice to remain either a common man or to activate the greatness sleeping within him and waiting to be activated.**

There are no common people; there are only common actions. Common actions are actions that are controlled by circumstances and environment. Material conditions should not determine an intelligent human being's living condition; rather, spiritual, and mental conditions should determine his material conditions. He should, through his ability to think, create the material conditions he wants for his life. **A person can lose all their possessions, however, if they have the right mindset, they can start again and attain success in no time.**

The power to become rich and a success comes from within. Ben saw the truth when all villagers of Fotetsa were fed, led, and misled by appearances. His ability to see through the ugliness of the place was not due to his privileged background or special abilities unique to him. Despite his small stature, he was able to transform an unknown village into a prime location and desirable hot spot.

He was able to bring wealth into a village that everyone had deserted due to poverty. The truth he perceived was immutable. He was able to tune into the supreme power within himself. Poverty takes charge where there is a separation between the inner self and spiritual aspirations.

When we start to look outwardly for solutions without searching for answers within us, we create a separation between ourselves and the divine in us; the source of all knowledge, the Holy Spirit. Any plans based on appearances, or on what we see, or perceive with our senses will bring no concrete results without insight. Any plans based on appearance will result in failure and deception. Where there is complete ignorance, and where the perceived truth is rooted in a false perception of realities, and where one longs for and chases after temporal things, the result will also be temporal.

If we can perceive beyond the senses and connect our mind with the hidden knowledge that is greater than our own, then, drawing from it, we will be inspired. This does not happen per chance or by mistake. We must be making a conscious demand to the world of ideas; that is, beyond changing appearances and mutable realities.

Each of us has God living within us, and this God is in whose image we are made. He is all truth, and all there is real. Whosoever links up to him through his spirit, will ultimately reach his goal.

He who remains continuously connected to God is able, at any time, to reach truths that can neither be explained nor denied.

A rebellious mind, or a mind that sees only what his senses can reveal, will see miracles in a rich man's achievements and realisation. An unruly mind refers to one who believes the only reality is the visible world. Those who are aware and who make an impact in any domain know quite well that the unseen governs the seen. Relying only on the five senses is foolish and self-limiting.

Ben had a limited education, but he had the power to perceive truths beyond the natural and the five senses. Ben always knew what he wanted and had the ability to determine the necessary steps to achieve his dreams. His achievements were not the result of his talent or supernatural power. His spirit just guided him. Each of us can emulate Ben. No one achieves their dreams by mistake. Each human being who finds their way can persevere in the face of adversity. You need to look from within to find your way. At any time, this is possible. Success is attainable.

Chapter 16

Now That We Understand, We Must Act

It is not enough to know what is required to get out of the pit. The most important thing is to get out of the pit. Africa is full of people who appear to have a solution for their problems and for everything else, but paradoxically, with all these know it all, the continent remains stagnant and has not progressed for years. If they truly knew, they should have put their theory to work. It is by its fruits that you will know a tree, says the Bible. What we see of Africans does not convince that they have a solution for their demise.

The number of good roads is decreasing in most countries. This is one area where an action is required. Corruption is growing and transmitted from father to child, and from generation to generation, action is also needed to tackle this issue. Students are all rhetoricians, perhaps they need to start practicing what they have learned. Each needs to search from within, for the pure truths, and when they find them, they must allow their thoughts to lead to solutions that can improve the continent.

I urge everyone to abandon everything that they have learned that does not solve their problems or which does not make their life easy and fulfilled. You that are reading now, I urge you to let your mind take control and guide you along your path. Your mind as ruler will create your material conditions. God is in you, and He will not lead you astray. You must surrender your body to the rulership of your mind. Do not listen to the forceful voice that is an echo of other people's will and purposes. You can discover who you are when you block out the distracting voices imposed on you from without.

Ensure that you understand your purpose, so you may fulfil it. Make a conscious effort to become aware of and recognise that the principle of power within you is real. The son is like the father; if you are the child of God, you have God's nature in you. You are therefore like God. You are the other, the alter-ego of God. Do not be afraid, it is real and you, with all these attributes, can be what you want to be. Start by recognising your worth, and consciously identify yourself with a higher power.

I suppose you didn't know that you were that powerful and able. Now you know how to exercise your rights and transform your mind, hence your life. Follow your dreams; abandon other people's dreams. Only your purpose will free you forever. You will only understand it if you take the time to listen to your infinite spiritual being. Trust not what you see, as it will fade. You need to believe only what you perceive as your actual destination. You will not get there if you do not believe in it. Have faith!

Ben, Ben of Melong, Mengang, Sekou, Dschang or Fotetsa or Ben of Saa' Nzock because his grandfather came from there? I am sure people from Fotetsa will claim him forever, as one of theirs, because he is an achiever. He trusted in his ability to be who he wanted to become, and he became. It does not matter where you come from; you can transform lives where you now live. You can choose where you call home, regardless of where you were born. You are not determined by your parents or your ancestor's background. It was just a place your great-grandfather happened to be when your grandfather was born. None of these places qualifies you. No matter where he is, Ben may call it home, and be in control of his life. He tamed the wildland Fotetsa, now the land of wonders. Through his will power and ability to think, he became a dominant figure in his country, where he is renowned and respected. He was not deterred by the desolation of the land he bought and transformed. He saw its worth beyond its superficial appearance. You need to understand the unlimited potential that you possess.

Chapter 17

Africa's Poverty: The Desired State of a Collective Subjective Mind

Everything has a spirit. The spirit of poverty solidifies, transforms, and manifests into a state of poverty. A vision and spirit of greatness transforms and displays a state of greatness. A human being, like a country or an organisation, has a spirit. Each entity or individualised spirit manifests into a physical appearance of its inner thoughts or reality. Generally, an individual reflects his spirit being, a pure reflection of his thoughts and a solidified state of their mental focus.

Unconsciously, we are deciding on what we should be. Unconsciously, we are creating our condition. Our mind is like a camera. What we focus on constantly will appear outwardly. What we let sink into our subconscious will appear outwardly and define our physical appearance and behaviour.

Since every structure or organisation has a spirit like humans, the spirit of an institution will be the reflection of that agency's leader's spirit, and to some extent, a projective identification of their inner being, transmitted through the organisation's culture.

An organisation's culture takes charge and dictates the conduct of its members. As such, success, or a failure of an organisation rests on how the organisation thinks. It is already clear from various management theories how a corporation thinks. An organisation's thoughts solidify and manifest into its observable position and performance, and its success is also a solidified form of the same spirit. An organisation that thinks that it is successful promotes success culture which therefore solidifies into an outward success of the same. Successful and companies are those who see success and their attribute. As such, the outward manifestation of an individual or organisation is greatly an exteriorisation of its subjective mind.

The subjective mind has no ability to refute what is projected in equally, it has no ability to reflect on what it receives. It receives in and projects exactly what it has received outwardly. The subjective mind accepts everything as it is channelled in, as reality and truth that should be, and always manifests outwardly what it receives through suggestions.

If you suggest, for example, that you are poor, your subjective mind will always reflect poverty in its outward manifestation. Furthermore, by just calling a child stupid or a criminal, his subjective mind will receive this suggestion as true, and it will, in the long run, manifest outwardly in the child's behaviour.

The more we quality African as poor and the more they opened their mind to receive such assertions, the more their subjective minds accept as such and reflects out what it has received. For example, when various medium is used to diminish Africa, it will feel inferiors and remained behind. Discourses, TV, radio, letters, conferences and through international organisations or co-operations are used to drum about African poverty and this sinks into African people's subconscious minds which register this in their subjective mind as true, and as the population internalises such assertions, it is projected outwardly in their behaviour. This is the reason why they ultimately think, see and accept poverty as a norm. Unless counter transferences are robust enough to reject such suggestions, each person exposed to such publicity will find it difficult to refute it.

The subjective mind doesn't have any sense of humour, can't understand tricks or jokes. The subjective mind is earnest and takes in everything as reality, without the ability to determine whether it is a joke or not, and what it takes in is manifested outwardly in the entity or individual's life. In essence, a subjective reality does not assume there is an external reality. This view holds that consciousness is all there is and that all consciousness is universal - that is, there are no pesky other minds to become a problem. Some will suggest that there is only one ultimate mind that is the source and originator of all subjective experiences, but whether one is entirely agreeable to this idea or not, it is hardly refutable that what you register in, reflects out.

What you think of constantly and declare and confess to yourself will become what you are or get.

Perhaps, this is the secret behind prayer. When we are praying, we are focussing, introjecting, suggesting our requests to our subjective mind and the universal consciousness, ["That God that is within you, if you are regenerated"] which is all there is, and will reflects out what is declared in. This is the act of creation. Pure creation is by decree, by words, hence man is, like God, a creator; he creates, and contributes to creating who and what he is and becoming.

It follows that an individual consciousness, which is at first self-observing, experiences the same, now manifests into outer appearance. This means that a person's inner being, or inner self, experiences its thoughts. This state of consciousness, though always present, is experienced by only a few individuals, with the majority only dimly aware of their inner self. A conscious effort is required to contact this part of self. This inner being is the source and creator, as well as experiencer, of individual existence.

Subjective realities only take as real what it experiences first-hand, since external or objective facts are not seen as a reliable report, coming from second-hand sources. Therefore, failure comes when people spend their time seeking outside of themselves, what is an appearance of the reality, created by others. An individual can enjoy a glimpse of external realities, but they will never possess them because they are neither inherently part of their reality nor permanent.

Unless you find yourself, your own desired path, and, through your consciousness, or revelation, how to make it happen, you will run after others in vain. Some people who don't believe there is a God, think that there aren't any other minds. that we just believe there are. However, no one will deny the existence of *their* mind. This also explains why we do not have direct access to other people' minds (like through mind melds or some other technology), because there's nothing yet scientifically or technologically available to access them, except ourselves. This school of thought is limited as we often wonder why some people can read our mind in some circumstances, even from afar. There is possible invisible link between individual mind and other minds.

Believers think that in each mind is the mind of God. They believe that God lives in man through the Holy Spirit. For Christians, particularly those called born again, when you accept Christ, you are thus adopted into God's family. Your acceptance of Christ gives you full access to God's presence, inheritance and consequently, God's mind. Hence, believers have the possibility to receive revelatory gifts such as the Word of Knowledge, the Word of Wisdom, and the Spirit of discernment. These gifts allow individuals to know what another person is thinking, to show you what is in their mind, and you may be able to know without anyone telling you the secrets they are hiding, that they have never told anyone. This is called revelation.

Another person's mind can be revealed to you. You can only enter this stage when you are regularly in tune with the pure spirit in you: The Holy Spirit. This is conditioned by your ability to concentrate, pray, and live a pure life. An advanced state of quiet and regular prayers will make you reach a state of "superior you" that you did not think you couldn't reach. This again refers to the ability to reach in; an act of consciousness that can be accessed through concentration- Quiet thoughts.

Each person who reach this stage will know the solution to issues including his problems and the right path to take, hence, if you know what to do most of the time, if you can get the right answers most of the time, you will hardly miss your way. If, when in need of material or finance, you have the right answer, your problem will be solved. In short, you will always have because you will know what to do to get what you need all the times. So, you will become a stranger to poverty and failure.

I conclude that everyone can become great if they wish. Every organisation can succeed if it wants. Each continent can excel if it wants. The conditions for success involve receiving, introjecting messages of achievement and rejecting messages of failure.

Africans should be rejecting the message of poverty that is projected into their minds and start considering themselves as successful people. They should reject, through countertransference every negative message against their continent or against themselves. Projecting thoughts of success will transform their outward experience and behaviour. To do so, they should develop a robust system of counter-transferences and enhance their self-belief. Self-doubt and inferiority complexes amongst Africans are greatly due to their subconscious programming. They should, by way to conscious act, reject such suggestions and constantly affirm their greatness and their superiority.

Since the slave trade and following imperialism and colonialism, Africans were so poorly treated that they ended up believing that they were inferior. This is not the case. The greatness that made them build pyramids is still within them. The skills that helped them discover and transform iron has not left them.

The wisdom and strategies that lead them to build highly organised kingdoms and well-known trade centres are still dormant in them. If you walk on a £50 banknote or squeeze it, it will not lose its value. If you stamp and walk on a £50 note, it may become dirty, squeezed and bent, but will not lose its worth. It can be made straight again, it can be cleaned and will remain the same, retain the same value and you can still use it to buy what it could buy after that.

Africans should forget about the past, knowing that they have been dirty, squeezed and frustrated, however, they should remember that they have not lost neither their worth or their value, and their past exploits should point to the greatness that they have within.

It is the Western superiority complex that has made Europeans look great. Each of their citizens, even the most backwards, consider themselves as superior and great, and the more they act and behave like great people, they more their subconscious register their self-suggestion of greatness as true and the more they behave outwardly as great and the more they are considered as such, even though people may criticise their zealous stance, they unconsciously accept and believe it. No matter how painful it may be to accept such as true at the beginning, you end up accommodating t it and tolerating and then admitting it as true as well. It has been suggested to your subconscious which as registered and project it as such.

A concept is an abstract idea representing the fundamental characteristics of what it represents. Concepts arise as abstractions or generalisations and from experience, or the result of a transformation of existing ideas. Henceforward, Africans should find the right concept to qualify themselves as great people. This approach will become the norm that will progressively solidify into a visible manifestation of Africans' greatness observable through their behaviour.

The present reality is that our conscious mind knows that Africans are equally as great as any other human being, but temporary awareness is never projected and suggested for long to our subconscious. To ensure that Africans' greatness is registered in everyone's subconscious, they should start acting with a high degree of confidence which great and superior beings possess. This should start with the rejection of aid programmes and dependency on imported solutions.

Africans must sever with the tendency to use imported solutions, goods and services, or at least, adopt a discriminated approach to external imports, and start using what is available in their land. They must also start developing and improving what they have, thus advertising their own merits, and the value of what they have, and continue to consider themselves as the best, even if some people may think otherwise. They must believe that they can do anything they want to do and can be anyone that they want to be. They need to form a belief that they are not poor. This idea needs to be crystallised into their subconscious, and the more they believe in it, the more they will develop a strong and constant suggestions until this becomes part of them and their habits. Once it becomes part of their habits, it will become their second nature, thus defining them. They need to transform their subjective mind of lowliness into a subjective mind of greatness.

No African likes how they are portrayed; if the story of who you are does not reflect who you want to be, you should shelve it and follow who you want to be to emerge. Because the things of the world are fluid to power within us, it is therefore through that same power within that we rule. External forms are not reliable or permanent - the way Africa looks now is not permanent but may remain so, as long as there is no inner concept to change this appearance to impose what should be.

The fluidity of things comes through individuals, and the power of each person rules that fluidity, creating at each stage, a solidified form that is conceived from within. What you conceive from within, and firmly believe to be true and feasible will materialise at some point and become visible.

Human beings are not physical beings living in a physical world. They are spiritual beings residing in a different realm of consciousness that determines their physical conditions. Forms are ruled and make the spiritual world possible. In other words, material things are governed by the spiritual realm. You should not live life as things were before or now, but rather live as you think they should be.

You should not only believe things because you see them, but instead, you should see things because you believe they will be as you have represented them in your mind- your spirit. Believe what you see in your spirit. How you think about things will form the molecules of your existence. So, if you want to manifest the molecules of money, the molecules of joy, the molecules of peace, you must believe that you can have each, and take actions to transform those ideas into realities.

You should not compromise who you want to be. You must be acutely aware of who you want to become and live that reality. You need to keep believing as you press on to accomplish all that you wish to achieve.

What we see of Africa is a compromise as if the only way to survive is to give up what one holds dear as values. Such behaviours emphasise a lack of personality, lack of consciousness of one's strengths abilities and potential. Life is about consciousness. You are not governed by things, because you have the power to make things happen. **Your life is a result of the manifestation of your consciousness, and consequently of your making.**

The world you see is just the world of appearances; the true, unchangeable, and creative world is invisible, and only accessible through your mind.

The key to freedom is inside of you. The key to success is inside of you. The causes of your failure are inside of you. An organisation will be as successful as the inner being of its principal leaders. Therefore another individual can transform a failing organisation or business.

A new chief executive can suddenly change a failing business. This shift occurs in the minds of its new leader, and the consciousness of this shift operates in its employees' minds, not in the physicality of the structure. Yes, they may reduce the number of departments, reshape the organisation's structure, but the real change is what employee experience within. Most of the times, the organisation will still look the same, employing the same people; the difference is that its employees now have a change of mindset.

Africans can manipulate people, they can borrow money to satisfy a budget, they can compromise to survive temporally, but this will never improve their situation if there is no radical change in their mindset and behavioural pattern. For, behaving in the same way will always produce the same outcomes.

The true change should take place within an individual and since change is inherent to a being, merely changing a president will not change the country, if the new president does not bring about a change in people's mindset. To change without, you must change within.

If for example, a new president brings about a change of citizens' mindset, a change of attitudes, mentalities as well as social and structural change will follow. Let us imagine that your inner mind is like a house. If your house is dirty, it will smell. With the door closed, people may not be able to see what is inside. Passer-by will only see the beautiful structure. However, it might be filthy and full of junk, and despite its appearance and beauty, it will smell, and people who pass by your house will sense that smell. However, if you clean your house, not only will people appreciate its beauty, but they will also feel its freshness, even without you changing any paint.

The dirt inside the house was manifesting outwardly, even though the smell was not permanent. It is the same thing with African's poverty. It can be seen now, but once a change in mindset occurs, a physical manifestation of wellness, opulence and success will follow.

What people see of Africa now is fluid, and it can change once a mindset transformation program has taken place. The name Africa for some individuals who have never been there is a synonym of poverty, scarcity, and inferiority. This is not because African people are inferior, poor in nature. Like any other human being, they have the same potential and ability to excel. What makes them poor is the combination of programs that belittle them as well as their self-inflicted poverty mentality. They have been, for over a century, projecting a consciousness of poverty, scarcity and inferiority, and the more they have accepted their inferiority- which is not true- the more they have readapted their behaviour to what they believe they are and the more they will become the same as they think.

The same causes produce the same effects. Once you start to see yourself as great, you will be great, but if you see yourself and inferior and poor, you will end up being substandard and poor.

Let us take another example of an adopted child who has a consciousness of belonging to the adopted family. He may not have the same DNA as other members of the family. However, the consciousness of belonging to that family will make them feel and behave very much as part of that family. But if you start to put in the child's mind that he does not belong to the family, once he starts to manifest a consciousness of separateness from that family, there will be a disintegration that will become visible to those who may not know anything about that family history.

How people perceive your relationship with your family depends on your consciousness vis-a-vis that family. How you appear to people depend on how you see yourself.

In essence, people end up seeing what you think. If you think that you are great, people will see greatness in you. If you believe that you are incapable, people will see your inability and incapacity in you. Chief executives, presidents and prime ministers are normal people like anyone else. They just have the confidence to see themselves as able individuals who can fulfil such responsibilities. If you do not believe in yourself, no one will believe in you.

The inferiority mindset is projected everywhere across Africa. I have seen few proud countries in Africa. Almost all African countries want to rely on international aid and aid programs, and international aid conditions force Africans to compromise and to adopt legislations that continue to contribute to their demise and self-belittlement.

African countries project the spirit of poverty into their citizen's subjective minds. This projection goes beyond individuals and affects African companies, both regional and continental African organisations. For example, the African Union sees itself as a poor organisation, and so it is. Hence, it cannot pay for its upkeep or operating budget.

A continental organisation working to unite the continent, and to promote its economic advancement cannot even pay for its operating budget. Only 30% of African Union's budget comes from the continent. It is housed in a borrowed building, or to be kind, in a gifted building. Why should a flagship organisation of the whole continent like the African Union surrender its authority, and its very reason for existing, in exchange of money to pay for it running a budget in order to survive? China funded the construction of its headquarters. In fact, each year, the organisation begs for money and receives about 70% of its budget from foreign countries and donors.

Despite the African Union's needs, its leaders are not ashamed to chant how the continent is rich. How can a rich continent turn into a begging continent? Why should this happen in the first place? Is it because resources could not be found within the continent to meet its needs? Far from it! The problem is down to its people's mindset. The organisation is not poor, but its leaders are mentally poor, and their poor mentality impacts upon the organisation's ability to attract the necessary funding from within the continent.

The leaders transferred their country's behaviour into the agency's; as a result, the organisation began to behave like its people. The incivility that exists in each country is transferred to the organisation. As no leader pays for their membership fee, no citizens want to pay their taxes. The spirit of embezzlement, a refusal to pay their taxes and a refusal to respect national institutions is transferred into a refusal to pay their membership fee and to comply with the African Union's charter and constitution. African leaders who change their constitution every day also want to change the governing rules for the continental organisation, and this brings instability and a total lack of respect for the rules like in their own countries. Like in each country, the members refuse to pay their contribution and the lack of contribution cripples the organisation.

Citizens who believe they are poor become poor. An organisation that believes it is poor becomes poor. This has been said a few times elsewhere already. The African Union, through the adoption of its member's mentality, becomes compromised and loses its independence. It deviates from its objectives by accepting a bribe-softly called gifts- from foreign nations, who now become the organisation's principal owners and rulers. So, some policies the organisation adopts are greatly in contradiction with organisation's prerogatives and ambitions.

The African Union is a spiritual entity because its form, structure, advancement, and functioning are spiritual concepts. These concepts project the collective subjective mind of its members.

The collective subjective mind of the organisation is hijacked by the spirit of its member and in the case of Africa and Africa Union, citizen's minds are subjected and hijacked by the spirit of poverty which in turn affects the organisation and the whole continent. The organisation's inability to rise above what is happening within the continent is not surprising. As explained at great length, members' states are the cause of the Union's failure.

Just as Africa's poverty is a self-imposed, self-made, Africa's poor institutions are also self-imposed structures because Africans have developed a consciousness of self-limitation and self-annihilation.

Africa will change when Africans develop the consciousness of freedom, ability, development, superiority, greatness, and richness. When they will develop a mentality of self-liberation.

The African Union is an excellent organisation, with great ambitions. However, its limitations make it difficult to live up to its expectations. This is a common self-imposed predicament. The organisation needs to determine what it wants to be and behave in such way that others will perceive it just as it should be. There is no doubt that Africans are as great as anyone else, but the difference is that other project and affirm their greatness, whereas the Africans profess their inferiority, hence the outward manifestation of what each professes. When the USA, for example, wants to go to the outer planets, they have no doubts that they will get there. Their subjective mind accepts this as a fact, and they focus their efforts on making this happen. They do not start by thinking about where the money will come from because they know that they can create and to generate money required for the project.

Conversely, Africans will not even think about such projects, let alone try to develop that consciousness. The results are visible, as they continue to remain behind great advancements are undertaken by those who believe in their ability to achieve such advancements. The state of the continent is the product of a collective thinking. Africans lend their minds to their countries. This is the truth! Each lends a poor mind to the country, and collectively they remain poor. What we see and hear of Africa is the outer manifestation of African's collective thinking.

Chapter 18

The Tragedy of Outward Living

As Ben's journey across Africa unveiled, after gaining their independence, many countries were lost and therefore didn't know how to improve inherited structures. The most painful observation was that prior to colonisation these countries were never gripped by hunger, neither did they ever depend on foreign aid. As people began to see them as inferiors, they were given free aid, free food, free hospitals, free education, free everything and these gifts became like opium. A sleeping pill that emptied them from their drive to will and to do, from their drive to achieved and work hard and from their drive to think. They began progressively to adopt European cultures and lifestyle but were still counting on the handouts.

Africans were gradually living on other people's agendas and plans. This made them strangers to themselves, unable to think for themselves, unable to plan their lives as they used to do, and as they wished, or to think independently as they were accustomed to.

They were made to think and behave as the West wanted. Sometimes, they were encouraged into laziness with handouts, called aid programs, and with these imported and foreign concepts and programmes, hunger and misery started to make its way and settle in the continent. Now, almost every African expects help and support from someone. When you speak with someone, and when you start to build a relationship with them, they expect a gift and some form of support, particularly if they consider you as better off.

Everywhere in Africa, the lack of money is what people use as an excuse for their apathy and suffering. Each poor African says that if they had the right amount of capital, they would do something better to change their lives. However, the same people spent billions importing foreign goods.

Despite having very fertile lands, Africans import more than they produce. Imported goods could have easily been produced locally. However, there are no efforts to break this circle. The culture of using foreign products and services furthers their dependence on imports, whether commodities, technology or services or systems. This attitude cannot solve their misery or poverty.

Any like-minded person knows that the solution is not to import, but to find a local lasting solution. If outward solution-seeking has not helped, it is, therefore, important to find a better solution elsewhere. Long-lasting solutions can only be found through a reflection; this means turning within. Knowing that you have a rich subsoil, great reserves or arable lands is not enough if your population of over 1 billion people cannot be fed.

Despite having millions of hectares of arable lands and sought-after resources, poverty continues to dictate its law all over Africa. Africans have not done much to get the best from their land; not because the land cannot feed them, but because they cannot find the best way to get the best from their lands. The land can give them whatever they want if they use their mind correctly.

The solution to hunger, poverty and misery is in the spirit, not in the land. Africa needs to change its focus from looking outwardly, to inwardly looking. It would be difficult to overcome hunger and poverty without knowing how to fend for themselves, to multiply their supply, to protect themselves and to replenish their land in every way possible.

To overcome their spiritual poverty, Africans need to master what some people have called the science of business, the science of reproduction and the science of warfare. The science of business is a strategic way to plan their sourcing, their demand and supply. This requires determining the best routes to the market, understanding which products or resources strategic, and which partners are to leverage, bottleneck or strategic.

The science of business is the art of knowing how to deal with others, how to add value to what you have, how to get the best deal always, and how to multiply and replenish your supplies. There are rules in business, most of which are not taught and cannot be taught at school. The real secret of business resides within the individual, and therefore each trade has its secret. The secret is mostly revealed through a divine insight.

Together, Africa has a consumer force of around billion people. If the continent stops looking somewhere else for answers to their problems, they will find the solutions to their problems in the land. The continent is wealthy and can become richer if there is a change of mindset, priorities, and focus.

In addition to the science of business, Africa also needs to master the science of warfare and the science of mating or multiplication and replenishment of their species. Each living being has an instinct for self-preservation. Depending on their geographical location, they adopt different strategies to survive and self-preserve. Human beings had to invent ways to protect themselves in a changing environment. They should have a secret for protection and self-preservation against their potential competitors.

You cannot protect yourself with your challengers' weapons, as they know the ins and outs of their arms. If you buy weapons from them, they will always be ahead of you. It is foolish to think that your enemy will sell you weapons that they don't have the ability to protect themselves against. In any case, if they are selling you their warfare arsenal, they know your stock, and they will always be better prepared than you are, in case you ever go to war against them. If you depend on someone for your protection, you cannot fight them. Africa depends on others for solutions to feed its people, for reproduction techniques, for discoveries and their protection.

Africans should think their way out of dependency and poverty, not work their way out. The power of their thoughts remains their only weapon to fight their way out of poverty, from dependency and domination.

Systems are products of thoughts, so if you uncover a system that is used to keep you dependent, you must think of a counter system for your freedom. In Africa, there is an urgent need to think harder because wisdom is key to success; it is the ability to make the right choices in any situation. It is not difficult to do this if you ask God for wisdom. Great wisdom lies within each person. The pure spirit, the perfect spirit of knowledge and unlimited ability is in each human being without exception.

It is possible to discover new and creative ways for the continent to feed and protect itself. Since poverty is mostly due to ignorance, confusion and the proclivity to follow other people's agendas, it becomes necessary to fight confusion, ignorance and followership that distracts.

Avoid living a life that is imposed by others, giving up one's priorities and uniqueness. Mastering the science of self-defence requires a change of mindset. You need to bulwark your mind against toxins that cause confusion and dispersion. Every creature fends for itself. British people-built castles and invented cannons, but they did not stop there as they moved on to even more sophisticated arsenals.

Does Africa have in place something unique with the secret known only to themselves? I am not sure. Are they prepared to defend themselves? He that cannot protect himself is a prey in waiting and will end up on someone's menu. Every creature knows how to identify its enemies. Every species has a strategy for fighting its enemies; some produce odours, some change colours to blend with the environment around, and some just play dead. What is Africa's defence secret?

The science of business is not about having degrees in business administration, or in accounting. Administering a business means working for someone else, Accounting is looking after someone's account. The science of business is the hidden secret of business principles and strategies that each race must have. This should be unique to individuals, contexts, and situations. Africans must have their key principles, and secrets about business strategies that are unique to themselves, and hard for others to understand.

People put emphasis on education and schools; however, the science of life improvement and the science of business are not taught in the conventional educational system. They are taught in the antechamber of close nit groups. A secret is not easily given up. Such a secret is power held by the people who rule the society.

In a conventional education, Africans should be training employment creators, rather than training job seekers. Training job seekers creates a state of unemployment. Any individual who comes out with a good idea is overwhelmed with a demand for his service. A countless number of people knock at the doors of inventors, creators, and thinkers for either solutions or jobs.

Followers have no choice but to accept any position given to them. Most job seekers are university graduates who should be thinking critically and developing solutions to problems. But the reality is that African graduates are bringing no solutions to critical problems. They are not interested in bringing any solutions to their problems. Instead, they just want to secure a job. Their position is what matters to them. Their immediate needs are the only item on their agenda. They call the world to the rescue, seeking solutions elsewhere. Their subconscious has been programmed as such.

Solutions to a Malaria or Ebola cure, solutions to road building, infrastructures and technology can be found on the continent. Since their independence, Africans have not reflected adequately on their lack of progress. Despite their physical independence, they are still mentally colonised. Fortunately, they can overcome all these setbacks, provided they develop a solution focused mindset. Answers can be found in Africa, and there are people to do so. African people can achieve anything they desire if they believe in themselves.

Sudan divided its people because they found petrol. However, petrol only brings in tiny drops of income. Now each one wants to rule there. No one cares about the people they all claim to love and represent. As the fight continues, people are frightened, and this instability reduces peoples' ability to thrive. In Burundi, as I write this book, people are struggling for power and killing each other. The situation may change in few years' time, but, nonetheless, these egoistic actions from the leaders would have adversely affected the citizens.

Everyone wants to live in the promised land. However, the promised lands do not always roll out a welcome carpet. There was a desert before Canaan, and the Israelites had to cross the desert on their way to Canaan. In between the desert and the promised land, the rock provided water for their survival. But the rock only released water when it was stroked with the rod of wisdom and belief. Obviously, Moses knew something that his followers ignored. The physical appearance of the rock was dried, but he perceived water in the rock with his spirit.

The mind is the headquarters of true and pure realities. It is pure because it has no material form yet, and it is a reality, as it exists in substance, in mind and can live forever.

The physical body in which the spirit lives, using the material substance, keeps the spirit captive. However, the spirit is not material and wants to express its nature. The spirit lives in a world of ideas, and ideas are realities that can be materialised. The spirit sees things before they exist in their material forms. For ideas can bring about prosperity. Any product of thoughts can be translated into physical or material form to bring about tangible benefits; otherwise, they will remain concepts. Concepts on their own are of no use to man.

The tangible returns of discoveries are products of pure realities that attract value, based on the perceived benefits to its users. Not every innovation will help everyone. However, the more useful and needed a discovery, the more valuable it is and the more it will generate material returns that can be accumulated and used as exchanges for other experiences. The more people believe they can benefit from your discovery, the richer you will become because they will pay for it.

Being rich is having enough capital to exchange for any experience you want. Sekou built a city when he started to trade his hens, sheep, and goods for what he wanted. Later, he used his capital to buy building materials and employ workers. What he exchanged did not precede his thoughts. Instead, he thought about how to build a stock of the commodities before starting the process. He thought about what materials he may need, and what to do with the materials before acquiring them.

Ben followed a similar process. At Dschang, he started growing a few crops, hens and other domestic animals which he exchanged for food until he had enough to exchange for money that he used to build his school. Ben did not become rich because he had anything more than any other individual in his country. He became rich because he used his mind correctly. He transformed the ideas in his mind into a physical reality. He conceived a new way of delivering learning and a new means of payment.

Wealth accumulation follows the principle of having something of value to offer and the more useful you are to people, the more they will pay you, and the more they pay you, the more wealth you will accumulate for yourself, the more and better experiences you can have in life.

When I talk about experiences, I am talking about the things that make you feel fulfilled. One person may wish to enjoy three holidays a year, while another may desire to have mansions. Some people want to enjoy exotic food and wear designer clothes. Equally, others like to have a combination of many things such as luxury cars, many houses, lots of savings and the freedom to enjoy fine dining.

In general, apart from a personal inclination to certain things as a symbol of wealth, most people follow the pattern imposed by society which is: Beautiful and big homes or houses in exclusive places, cars and money in the bank, etc.

No one with mental abilities is limited. Only poor health can temporally hinder an individual's ability to do well. People may become ill after they have started a successful business, but if they have systems in place to keep their business going, the owner will still accumulate wealth, even during the period of illness. On the contrary, he who becomes ill before setting up a cash-generating system may be forced into poverty.

Even with limitations such as a handicap, man can still draw inspiration from other people to produce something of worth. He just needs to think about how he can be useful to others and what, in his mind, has the potential to solve existing problems. Once he has come out with an idea that can help people solve a common problem, people will pay for it. It is important to have capital, but capital is not always in monetary form. Without any financial capital one can, if he applies his mind well, find others who may accompany him on his dream and vision.

The first human discovered how to light a fire and created the necessary tools that he needed to survive. One good idea did not stop him from pursuing better ideas. Humans have kept pursuing ideas until they reached the industrial revolution, and more recently, the information and communication technological revolution. The road is still long.

While we presume that the path is still long, other people have already concluded that there is nothing more beyond the sky, or that nothing new can be discovered. This is a limited way of thinking. Some people think that individuals who are ahead have robbed them of their future or cheated them, so they cannot advance. This is not true. If by ruse or trick you are misguided, through a sound application of your thoughts, you can find your way back to the right path. No system is without a weakest point. To overcome such a point, you need to use your mind.

Man had surpassed horsepower, and machines now produce a million times better what in olden times when production was based on the workforce. Now, any physical force on offer will attract a low valuation. Hence, our society has already stratified and classified professions. How much you earn depends on what you do. Only those who make important decisions are well paid. Directors and chief executives do no physical work. They spend their time in meetings but get paid a thousand times more than a cleaner. Here again, it is about how the mind is used to solve problems. Decision-making is problem-solving. He who uses his mind better attracts the biggest pay cheque. Nothing confines anyone to one category of business or another. Nothing restricts a man to either poverty or wealth but that man himself. Each may stay in a class by choice and can leave it by choice at any time. Many people have changed their lives after being unhappy with their situation.

Those who are limited by what they see and taste, those who base their experience and efforts in pursuing phenomenon have no difficulties with struggle. In fact, a struggle is an inevitable outcome for them. They barely bring about lasting changes in human's experience and fulfilment, so they receive less for what they, if anything at all, bring to the rendezvous of giving and receiving. As they develop fewer solutions to human problems, they receive fewer rewards. Consequently, they remain poor.

True knowledge cannot be empirical because what is empirical is temporal, mutable and changeable. But what is spiritual cannot change and cannot finish or end. Therefore, a rich man may lose his wealth but will eventually become rich again if he wishes. He knows the process of getting rich; the concept and process are in his mind so that he can replicate his success at will.

But a poor man who, by acts of fraud, hard work or fortune gathers wealth, may return to poverty when he has spent all his money, or when he has lost his physical abilities for working hard. Most hard workers remain poor when they grow older, but most smart employees become rich when they age. The latter category uses the power of their thoughts to create systems or services that bring value to others, thus perpetuating their income while they are asleep.

One good problem solved will generate enough revenue for a lifetime, and sufficient reserves to leave a legacy. I have never seen any place other than Africa, where people work hard every day, but barely eat two meals a day. Subsistence farmers are always on their farms, doing the same things their ancestors did hundred years ago, with the same instruments - machetes and hoes – planting the same crops, in the same way, and obtaining the same results. They don't have enough to feed themselves, so they cannot generate a surplus. They don't know how to generate a surplus, and they don't know because they have no idea how to create value from what they have. They can never change their status or social position without changing their mindset.

A mental revolution will precede a social revolution because a change of social system may not necessarily change people's mindsets unless it is focused on such. You can build skyscrapers and roads, but people will still want to go back to that which they have been naturally and unconsciously programmed to be. Their subconscious and unconscious dictate their behaviour. Whosoever should understand the power of the unconscious mind, would understand the self, hence their unlimited power to be and do whatever they wish in this world.

Jesus, in the Bible, didn't do any miracles in Jerusalem, because of their non-belief. They didn't believe miracles were possible, particularly from Jesus, whom they knew well. So, nothing happened to them. However, those who embraced new ideas, whose mental disposition was to believe all things were possible, received miracles. They saw possibilities and embraced them. They changed their mindset, and that is all that Jesus Christ was telling people to do: "Change the way you think, about God, about the world and about what you have been taught about yourself". "Change your mindset". God was no longer a fearsome person, but someone who could help and love unconditionally. So, he was in each human being, and by linking our thoughts to him- the Holy Spirit- we can perceive the truth, and pure realities will be revealed to us and set us free forever.

The lack of self-confidence in Africa is behind the slow progress of the continent. Most Africans are convinced that on their own, they cannot change anything. They believe that they cannot influence the world, let alone change it. Where people believed the change was possible, change followed, and where they believed in success and achievement, great things happened.

A firm belief, otherwise called faith, triggers something within the subconscious mind that brings about the expected result. The unconscious mind consists of the automatically occurring processes that are available through introspection. These methods include thought processes, memories, interests, and motivations. Unconsciously, peoples' mindsets can be tuned to success or failure.

Success-seeking opportunities generate success, progress and achievement. Where People believe in possibilities, possibilities open to them and become visible. Possibilities are not created by themselves, but by people. A man is the creator of possibilities, and to believe there could be something called an iron, it already knows what iron is and a possible utility of iron, and, subsequently what could be done with it.

Once a concept is conceived, the possibility of turning it into a real form becomes possible. Iron is a mineral, and gold is only a rock. Petroleum can only be found amidst water and looks like mud, but those who made these commodities useful first saw through these rocks, and this mud, to their possible importance, usefulness, and utilities.

Someone sees a seed as good for food, but another sees in a seed a tree, and beyond a tree a forest and subsequently, a beautiful window frame, a king size bed, a well-polished furniture and a Louis IV chair.

Those who have eaten the seed will never have neither the bed or the chairs or the window frames.

So, beyond the natural, there is a spirit that sees forms and beauty beyond sensual perceptions. This is the power latent in every human. The ability to decide what a thing should be, compared to what it is here and now, is crucial to progress, achievement and wealth creation. This is called added value, and each of us can increase the value to something.

The infinite power to transform the world in which we live is in each of us. From within ourselves, we can draw from the immutable substance, immutable realities, and truths.

The fight for gold, diamonds and timbers is useless because more resources can be found with the right application of thought processes. A good researcher needs a quiet space and time to think and reflect.

It follows that gunfire is a threat to calm thinking and systematic application cf thoughts. **In a time of peace, it is possible to discover more resources and possibilities. Stability offers greater opportunities to explore or improve on things already at hand, or to create and transform the whole country and continent's experience. But chaos can only reduce possibilities and the ability to concentrate. With concentration, each is a potential inventor, creator, discoverer, improver, innovator, and transformer.**

Each human being is here to solve a problem. If you miss your problem, you will go unnoticed. We know about Plato, Ramses, and Archimedes because they sought answers to profound questions about life, society, natural laws, architecture, or arithmetical problems, and they solved those problems. Each of these figures attracted followers whose lives were enriched in many ways.

We have the concrete and the abstract. The concrete can change anytime, depending on the weather, atmospheric pressure. The abstract doesn't change and determines what the concrete will become. The abstract rules the concrete. The abstract is forever true and real.

You cannot touch mathematical, chemistry or physics formulas, yet their application determines the outcomes of physical forms. These formulas do not derive from the concrete; they are pure products of thoughts and are the result of a mindset. **Only those who can perceive the abstract can find their concrete application, and wealth accumulation follows a sound application of thoughts**. Thinking also helps to make life easier and opens opportunities for various experiences.

Wealth and poverty are experiences; scarcity creates poverty, which brings experience of suffering and destitution, while wealth leads to abundance and fulfilment. Wealth or poverty can be measured in monetary equivalent.

Excessive accumulation of lack of insight creates penury, lack, deprivation, and poverty. On the contrary, excessive accumulation of the real- the abstract- will lead to wealth, and its legal protection, which is an indication of insight. This is called the intellectual property, and people protect their intellectual properties, which attract loyalties. The payment of loyalties brings money, translatable into accumulative concrete returns, hence, wealth and legacy.

The Western world understood the importance of protecting their brain children. They understood the importance of protecting their intellectual properties. Nowadays, most investors, even though they may be dead, still receive royalties from their discoveries and inventions. This is proof that, if you solve concrete human problems and protect your discoveries, you will attract financial benefits.

Man cannot be happy if he is hungry or ill. Poverty distracts the spirit and prevents it

from thriving. No matter what some people may say, no one is happy in poverty or destitution, because they are double trouble, both in flesh-body and in spirit. Instead of looking elsewhere, tune in for answers. You can solve the mysteries of lack and scantiness.

Chapter 19

Quality Thinking Leads to Quality Living

How much money can you make from a poor man? He that has nothing is unable to keep the littlest drops that may come his way. He always has nothing or not much. He that has more can keep some reserves for a bit longer, and can accumulate harvest upon harvest, and can be trusted with more. A poor man has no reserves. A rich man may not have any reserves of material possessions, but he can also create wealth at any time he wishes using his abundant mental reserves. By applying the same science, he has used in the past to accumulate wealth, he will achieve the same or better results.

There is no poor land anywhere in the world. Every corner of the earth is rich in its own way. There are only poor minds living in untamed lands across the world. There are no poor lands in Africa. Africa is only full of people with poor mindsets.

If Africans change the way they think, their land will change its offerings. If they change their mindset, they will change their lives. If they change their behaviour, they will change their value. If they change their thought processes, they will become wealthy. To change the way of life, they need to change the way they think.

Let's take one example: At the beginning of an experience, you select two countries, let say Belgium and Congo, and ask them to voluntarily swap countries, whereby, Congolese will be moved to Belgium and Belgians to Congo. You will notice that all Congolese would want to migrate to Belgium, whereas Belgians would prefer to remain in their country. But let us force the Belgians to move to Congo and agree for Congolese to also move to Belgium. (Please note that this is just an example, applicable to any countries where people only focus on material things without knowing how others managed to produce them. I am trying to illustrate how a good thinker can change his world, no matter where he finds himself).

Each group remains in their new country for 20 years. After the 20 years, the people from Belgium who moved over to the Congo would have changed, and Congo also would have changed for better. Equally, the people of Congo who were transferred to Belgium would have physically changed, and Belgium would have also changed, but for worse. After 20 years of Belgian migration, the Congo would have started to look like Belgium; and likewise, Belgium would have started to look like the Congo before the swap.

Now, we go back to the same people and ask each of them to return to their original countries. While the Congolese would want to go back to their original land, the Belgians would want to stay in Congo and continue the transformation of the Congo. The Congolese would start to reject Belgium, and would not hesitate to claim back their land, even by force, and may even argue that they were duped to go to Belgium, even though they volunteered to move there.

If we check the two countries now, we will see that upon their arrival in Belgium, the Congolese quickly used everything that they found there. They would have enjoyed the roads, the houses, the food, and they would have managed companies without maintaining them. The food and reserves would have been used up, without any planning for the future.

The environment would now look untidy and dilapidated, exactly like the Congo they left behind. Conversely, the Congo under the Belgians would have transformed and progressively become like the Belgium they left behind.

This experience shows that the Congolese would have moved with their culture and habits. They would have enjoyed emptying the land without replenishing it or undertaking any improvements, as they did back in Congo. However, the Belgians, who initially didn't want to move to Congo, would have transformed the country to their liking, based on their Belgian model. Belgians would also have moved to Congo with their culture and mindset.

These behaviours are the real picture of what would happen in such circumstances. Congolese have remained Congolese, even in a place they initially considered to be a paradise, without changing their mindset, they would have progressively transformed the paradise into a derelict, impoverished, neglected land as their country-Congo.

The Belgians would have suffered at the beginning of their resettlement in Congo but would have started to replicate their lifestyle in the same way they did back in Belgium, and the neglected, old and almost disintegrating Congo would have begun to be as beautiful as Belgium. Why would this happen? This would happen because each group has a mindset, and the land transformation for the worse or good reflects how each group thinks and behave.

The state of a place reflects the state of mind of its inhabitants. Habits, as we have already said, determine our actions and our way of life. **The concept of chaos or order is in the mind and not in the land. Likewise, the ability to improve one's life is in the spirit, not in the land.**

People blame the crumbling African infrastructure on the lack of resources and money, but if you give that same land to other people, with the same income string that Africa has now, they will transform it without bringing any extra resources or money from anywhere else.

Poor people are quick to see no future in a seed. To them, a seed only represents food. They see in a seed no possible garden or farm and no ultimate source for food. Rich people see in a seed the potential for an uninterrupted supply.

The Congolese's eagerness to move to Belgium was motivated by the physical appearance of Belgium. They ignored that Belgium's infrastructures were not what made Belgium great. Belgians made Belgium great, and their spirit of achievement was essential to building their infrastructures and not the contrary.

Africans make Africa poor, not the contrary. What is perceived with the five senses is never permanent; rather this reality is in a constant state of flux. Improvements are only made possible by imagination and creativity.

The Congolese did not want Belgium; rather, they wanted the Belgian way of life. In contrast, Belgians never desired the Congolese way of life. This is the reason why one group wanted to move to the new country, and the other wanted to stay in their land.

The Belgians knew who they were, and they remained themselves whilst in Congo where they replicated their way of life. The Congolese, not knowing who they are desired envying in the Belgians' lifestyle without knowing how they built their country. Once in Belgium, they sucked out any Belgian substance in the Belgian environment, then everted to their Congolese way of life. They got stuck, not knowing what to do next. Once they finished what could be grasp, their spirit of poverty resurged. They wanted to return to their land once they knew it had been transformed.

This further confirms that poor people do not live their own lives. They are always trying to live other people's lives. They live "borrowed lives" with a "borrowed-self", annihilation, and self-resignation. This can be translated into a theory when this observation is put into a greater context of nations.

If we take the axiom of the northern and southern hemispheres, there will be a common trait amongst people from the northern hemisphere and a common trait amongst people from the southern hemisphere, excluding the east side of the south- I am talking about Australia and Newzeland. I mean that there is a common trait between Africans and a common trait between Europeans. These traits are a consequence of the type of education system developed in each continent. The educational system is then combined with their views of the world.

Where more efforts are put into producing effective and quality minds, the whole nation benefits. Where there are quality thinkers, there is a better quality of life. Quality thinkers create quality life, abundant material and wealth, and consequently richer nations and citizens.

The conditions of any society are determined by the intellectual and spiritual capacities of its citizens. So, the transformation of any country starts with the conversion of its citizens' minds. To transform society, we need to change citizen's minds.

Quality thinkers produce quality life, quality nations and consequently quality people around them. This point has already been made, and here is just a reminder! Ben changed the mindset of people of Fotetsa and influenced a whole generation. Quality thinkers are also world changers. Quality thinkers decide the world's outlook. Individuals who have dominated the world started by conditioning other people's minds. You may provide for people all the time to help them avoid poverty, but they will remain poor unless they rid themselves of the poverty mentality. Every rich nation has people who think for the country's future.

Outwardly struggling people are those whose minds are struggling to find solutions to their plight. A struggling mind is an unstable and poor mind. Struggling minds create struggling nations. A prosperous nation is full of good thinkers, whose ideas generate ideas and wealth.

Some countries are already thinking about what they will do in 50- and 100-years' time, while others are still thinking about how they will survive today. Struggling nations do not think beyond the next election term. **Their citizens, ignoring that each creates his conditions, continue to look to failing governments for answers to their problems.**

What can a confused and failing government offer its citizens, apart from uncertainty and despair? Failing governments are confused, leading their citizens to perdition. A failing government creates a weak system, and a failing system, de facto, creates a declining society full of failing and disillusioned citizens.

A falling educational system will fail pupils, thus derail a whole generation, apart from those who trust more in their own abilities. Each person has this capacity, but in the absence of an active mind, it's hard to detach themselves from what they have been regularly presented as the norm.

A child will continue to mimic his parents unless he makes a conscious decision to separate himself from what his parents tell him. Few people have the willingness to seek advice from within. Many individuals will always follow the crowd and what is popular. What is popular is neither right nor real. The world is full of people who follow the popular, the unreal, the shadows. Therefore, the majority of the world's inhabitants are poor. They are poor because they are following, instead of being leaders in their fields. The original is always the real. A copy is a copy and depending on how close or remote it is from the original, a copy can be entirely distorted, and end up looking nothing at all like the original.

Africans are copycats, trying to live like people who are over 7000 miles away from them, living in different weather, guided by a different mindset. This is the reason why Africa is failing.

People are attracted to richer nations without understanding how they became wealthy. They want to import material goods into their countries, without a plan for creating those desired items at home. Without a sustainable plan to produce most of what they need, they will never have freedom or real advancement. They would keep on transferring the little income they have abroad to buy things that, if they wanted, they could have produced themselves. It is disheartening, and a voice is shouting within as I write. I hear this chant: CHANGE YOUR MIND-SET IF YOU WANT TO CHANGE YOU LIFE. CHANGE YOUR THOUGHTS IF YOU WANT TO CHANGE YOUR FORTUNE. CHANGE WITHIN TO CHANGE WITHOUT! YOU ARE EQUALLY ABLE. YOU ARE A CREATOR. YOU CAN MAKE OF YOUR COUNTRY WHAT YOU WANT IT TO BECOME.

You are crying every day that you have been colonised, fooled, and robbed, but you are unconsciously perpetrating your demise. Nothing outside of your spiritual being is real or permanent. What you see will fade; what you have within will not. Whatever you imagine, you can create. See, in your mind, how you want your land to become, and seek in your mind the path to get there, starting with small steps until you can jump.

Do not just jump! Where will you land if you jump without knowing your landing platform? Do not jump because others are jumping; they know their destination and their landing platform. They have jumped on you and will land on safe ground, but you will land on the dangerous ground because they would have occupied the full platform and the best spot before your arrival. You can create your landing platform otherwise; you will always be behind if you are a follower.

You will always be far away from the perfect spot, and the honorary table, as a follower. You will always hear the echoes because you are far from the music source. You will always be left with the crumbs because no one will deprive his children for you. So, you may never taste real food, if you sit and wait for what others have produced. So, why are you complaining if you cannot assess the reasons behind your failure?

You are as able as any other human being. Why wait for West to lead the way in everything?

Find your route(s), find your strengths, and find your purpose. What is best for others is not necessarily best for you. Find what is right for you, by yourself. The solution is in you, not in others. Your mind is not shared with others. Your inner mind can never fully be understood by others, and you may never translate into words what you know and see from within; however, you can make the most of what you think to make things happen.

Your feelings cannot be felt by anyone else but you. Others can only guess what may be going on within you. What your imagination can discover is already real. Do not be afraid; you can make it happen. You are a miracle. You are a creator, but you will not create anything without using your creative power, and this power is in you. Look inwardly; you will find it. Without the real, you are acting.

You are a spirit, and only your mind can determine what you do with your body. If you want to treat your body, first heal your mind, because it is the real you. If you neglect the real you, you will suffer. As you fly in spirit, you can fly in the body. It is possible, provided you doubt not!

Chapter 20

All is at Hand; Let Us Justify Our Presence Here.

The crowd was uncontrollable, each shouting as loud as they could; they were all in a hurry, going who knows where. In this melting pot of noise and confusion, a helpless woman fumbled through the scores of bags she carried, as she tried to tick off a list with a pen clenched between her teeth. As she saw the young man rush past, she gathered her strength and called out to him. However, the young man could not hear her above the chaos. Did she know him and what did she want with him? The answer remained a mystery to Ben as he stood by watching. The hot tropical sun continued to warm as the stinking air smelled of sweat and rotten fish.

This scenario took place over forty years ago when Ben was still a child. Now wealthy and renowned, he had returned to visit the same market in Mengang. Some of the market traders he knew had grown up and were now assisted by their children. Not a lot had changed, except Rimtounda had died, but his shop had not closed. His children had learned the trade from their dad and were continuing in the same line. It had become a profession for three of his children. Each had opened their brewery next to each other, as they continued to struggle to share a limited clientele. None of them had a dream beyond the village or to industrialise their secret brew. None of them dreamed of leaving Mengang. To them, Mengang was all the world was. The horizon was the limit, and the farthest they knew was the next village. The only language they knew was theirs. They would probably live like their father and die without making any influence or any impact on people's lives, except getting them drunk. They would have lived and died, just like their father. This is common to common people.

Odontol, a 100% pure alcohol, was now more widespread than before. People continued to pay the price for overdosing on this drink: it affected their teeth and caused heart attacks and even sudden death. Market stalls were degrading, but no one appeared to care, as, for them, life was normal this way.

Ben proceeded to their old compound. The livestock they had left disappeared just after their departure. The new occupants of their old house had changed nothing on the house they were expelled from. In fact, the house had aged and was crumbling. The village, in general, looked poorer than before. What had happened to what they left behind after being expelled from the village?

From their old compound, Ben proceeded to pay a visit to the king who, only a few years ago, was invited to the grand opening of his castle. The king recognised him. He was excited and screaming like a little child as he alerted the whole village. Soon, the entire village was gathered at the king's palace to welcome Ben.

Women were singing, children were jumping, and men were chatting. It was a feast, and Ben offered them all sorts of gifts that he came with. He had forgotten no one. Aided by his assistants, sweets, bread, oil, food, meat, cloth and shoes were distributed. Each villager received more than they ever had in their life, in one day.

Despite the unexpected visit and unexpected gifts, the villagers still had a lot to ask. The surprise visit with unexpected gifts did not satisfy them. They still had a lot of needs that they hoped Ben would help them fulfil. Before formulating their requests, they began talking at once: "This is our very own son"; "You are a son of this village and will always remain one of ours, and we thank you for showing us love when you could have been seeking revenge". "You are showing us love and peace and kindness, despite the hurts of the past. You are truly exceptional, and we can't thank you enough."

As a gesture of returned kindness, the king offered him another piece of land, which he turned down. Ben had more than enough.

As he sat there amidst his hosts, plenty of requests were formulated. Many wanted help to send their children to school; others wanted him to pay for their medical treatment or repair a run-down school of the village. Young people wanted to follow him wherever he went. Like in most parts of Africa, few people had something to do. The usual claim was, there are no jobs here in the village, and there is not much to do here!

Ben offered to build a brand-new school and a medical centre in the village. This was the most surprising. Ben was changing the face of Mengang, thanks to money. Who said that money is not good? For such people, Ben showed that with more than enough, you can also do more for yourself and for the needy.

Ben was showing that having a low-income family background does not prevent one from achieving much in life. Ben was a living example of what man can become if he wishes. Perhaps, he will inspire the younger generation in this village. Up till then, no one from Mengang had ever done anything noteworthy. Life was nothing but struggle, pain and suffering for some people. This was the language everyone used in this part of the world. No wonder they were not moving beyond their current circumstances. In this part of the world, having enough to eat was the most pressing concern, and doing so was a luxury. Eating enough meant living well.

Success was measured by how much and how many times someone could afford to eat each day. Those who ate every day were considered rich and admired by all. It was mind-blowing to see how a man with unlimited potential could think so low! Did they ever wonder who discovered drugs, cars, and even the simple petrol lamps they used in the village? Given that they were still using the same tools as their ancestors, perhaps they did not give much consideration to new inventions.

Mengang was no different from Akosombo in Ghana, Tenkodogo in Burkina Faso, or Sinkanse in Togo. People behaved the same. They had the same concerns: to be able to eat. In every part of the world where people spend the majority of their time trying to feed themselves, progress is slow. Each person whose priority is to feed himself will hardly influence the world.

Throughout Africa, most people either did not believe that they could be of help to the world, or that they were exceptional. Few people believed they had a great destiny and were able to change lives. For most of those languishing in poverty, it was a matter of finding someone per chance or fortune, who could improve their living conditions. Begging was the ultimate choice for all, and poverty was each one's attribute. They had opted and conditioned their minds to think, behave and accept poverty as a norm.

If they could understand that each of them had the same potential as Ben, perhaps they would have tried something new. It was possible for each of these people to achieve more than being born, living only to survive, and dying.

If everyone lived like this, there would be no doctors, and if there were no doctors, there would be no medicine or new technology to improve lives; life would be worse off. In the middle of a rich and diverse land, we find the poorest people on earth. This proves that it is not so much about what is in the land, but rather it is about what the people of the land did with their minds. They were able and could command the land to bring forth what they wanted if they used their mind well. What a shame. Wasted lives with wasted minds, and potential that would never manifest.

Each is responsible for self and to the world. Poverty is a state of mind rather than a state of a place. Any place, anywhere in the world, can change its fortune if people are willing to put in the efforts. People can make of a place what they want. A paradise can be created in the middle of a jungle; likewise, a thriving and vibrant city can be transformed into a desolate land through man's actions. Thoughts guide such actions. People wanted to build the tower of Babel and God believed they could do it. Man can do anything he sets his mind to.

It is a shame that, so many lives go to waste. It is also a shame that Africans always wonder why things don't go their way. So, for things to go your way, you need to make them go in that direction. Think about what you need to do, and make it happen. We may accuse people of exploiting Africa's resources, but the causes are deeper than the exploitation of resources. First, Africans did not discover those resources, and if they did, they made no efforts to make good use of them, and they didn't know what to do with them; hence, since their discovery, they have not done anything to transform them by themselves. They have also not made the new discoveries that the world craves after. It is easy to complain like I once did, but with time, it is logical to conclude that each society creates its conditions, whether for wealth or poverty.

The land is as rich as its people. The way people think will determine the way they live. Because human beings are essentially a progressive species, the deeper their thoughts, the more creative they can be. Creativity enables people to see value in a land, in a product or in a resource.

There are resources, I am sure, that are yet to be discovered. We have not discovered them yet, perhaps because we do not know about their nature or utility. A creative mind will discover and find a new way to use them. As a result, the whole human race will benefit.

People need to go beyond eating, drinking and being merry. Over-excitement reduces our ability to think. Thinking is a prerequisite to conceiving lasting solutions to life, pressing the issue. Poverty can only be overcome when an individual makes good use of his mind. Every product, service and institution began as an idea in someone's mind. Trying to find solutions outside one's thought process means exposure to distraction, noise, and confusion. Find solutions that can influence systems to come from within. You cannot overcome poverty if you cannot comprehend yourself, and to comprehend yourself, you should strive to come to terms with your thoughts, and how you can apply them to solve problems.

There is no limit to what man can do; there is no set time or age for a change of a mindset. A shift in mindset will create a shift in your life. You may have grown up in a slum, believing you will always be poor, but if you change your belief system, you will soon notice a difference in your life. You are different from people living around you.

When you begin to understand that you are different from others, when you engage in the process of self-discovery, you will notice a difference between you and others, through introspection and reflection, and this is the beginning of consciousness. Although you may have been inspired by something external, real change comes from within you.

It is only from within that you will understand that something has touched you, and called you to change, something in you that has aroused to show you that you have a tremendous dormant and potential power that you did not know that you possessed. Everyone, including Kweku from Ghana and Diouf from Senegal has it.

But not everyone knows at birth or growing up that they are great. Most societies and cultures tend to teach that man he is limited, not perfect, and this makes each child think of themselves as limited. To some extent, it makes them believe that they are unable to achieve anything beyond the ordinary.

Some people discover earlier in life who they are, but others struggle to come to terms with it. Many will never discover who they truly are and will never realise their potential. However, once you are conscious of what is in you and take a firm decision to release it, you begin to remove all traits of self-limitation and can achieve something exceptional. Only those who do something exceptional are renowned and distinguished.

Those who have made a difference in their environment are remembered. Each person can make a difference, and the difference they make justifies their presence here on earth. This cannot be done without the efficient use of one's mind. It is therefore important to take care of what goes into your mind. The greater the thoughts that go into your mind, the greater the possible outputs.

By your own making, you can make a great individual out of yourself. Think like you are your own capital. As such, you want to yield great returns. You have a choice as to where to deposit your capital: at a bank where your capital will shrink, or at a bank that embraces innovation and creative thinking capable of producing great returns.

You are a great asset to yourself and the world. You need to first see yourself as such, and then find an area where your great potential can be unleashed.

Once you unleash your potential, you will be noticed, and thereby justify your presence on earth. Remember that an aeroplane was once only an idea in one's mind. I am sure many people had this idea, but only the Wright brothers tried it first. No matter the invention- even those that may look trivial- they all meet someone's needs. Have you thought about who invented the bed?

Human beings are still in need of other things that will improve their lives. Many discoveries still need to be made. Look at your environment with an enquiring mind to determine what problem you can solve. This is what will make you and explain why you were placed on earth.

Chapter 21

Your Subconscious Holds the Secret to your Success.

ANYTHING THAT WE CAN DO WITH EASE HAS ENTERED OUR SUBCONSCIOUS. THE OUTER MANIFESTATION OF OUR ACTION OR BEHAVIOUR IS JUST A REPLICA OF WHAT IS WITHIN US. As a result of regular practice, a musician needs not look at the notes before playing. A good driver no longer looks at the brakes or the accelerator; he knows where each pedal is without looking. This law is true and simple; but we fail to realise that it applies to every sphere of our life.

Success or failure can be a slow and long learning process that has sunk into our subconscious. The outward manifestation of success, what people see in a successful person' display, is only an unfolding of what he has registered in his subconscious and acknowledged as truths over the years. It is the principle that he has integrated and accepted through a learning process. It is what he has believed and deemed possible. There are people who will never play a musical instrument. They find it difficult to memorise a single note. There are people who will never drive a car despite learning or trying to learn how to drive. They find it complicated and believe they cannot drive- so, they are unable to drive. The truth you tell yourself is the truth your subconscious records and projects out as a behaviour you display.

What you think and believe is what is! You cannot think of good and display a bad behaviour. To be genuinely good from without, you have to be good from within even though one can pretend to be good from without being good from within.

The ability of an individual to think is a way by which he can enact and impose his will on earth, thus changing his conditions. An individual's impact on nature can only be effective if he uses his power within. His power and ability to think lead to self-discovery. Human consciousness consists of his ability to think. Descartes said that man is a being whose essence is to think. Man is "a thinking being".

This activity of the mind is dynamic and not static; as such, it can adapt, draw inspiration, and learn new things. Positive learning will influence inspiration, and the subconscious will register these positive thoughts, and reflect them outwardly as a positive manifestation of needs and wants. Pure inspiration and pure forms can only be drawn from eternal and immutable forms through human' mind. Man's ability to tap into the "cmnipotent" mind– enables him to conceive ideas without limits. The universe is infinite; so is the mind, and man can think like God. Each human has a mind that has no limits as to how far it can perceive things that are not yet visible or in existence, but what is perceived clearly in the mind can be made existent in the physical realm with a burning desire and an unfailing will to make it happen. This is true, but only few use their mind like they should or consider it as a source for their limitless ability.

Every individual can do the impossible, but few people try the impossible. Each can achieve far beyond what the eyes can see, or what the senses can experience, but few people want to go beyond what they see, smell, feel, taste or hear. They live by their senses, so the changing weather changes their perception of the world and they end up living with false realities and preconceptions.

Your first duty to God, to yourself, and to the world is to make yourself great, to succeed and to achieve beyond what is naturally expected of you. **The God in you rejects poverty; therefore, you will never be happy with scarcity. Fortunately, you can change and be who you want to be, only if you are willing.**

You can have as much as you want to have if you use your mind correctly. Your ability to create wealth resides within you, and the world within commands the world without. **From within, you can effect change without. From within you cause things that will affect the visible world, the sensory world. The cause is within; the effect is without. The cause is unseen, and the effect is visible. An invisible cause triggers a visible effect.**

The causes of poverty are invisible, but its effects are apparent and observable. It follows that those who respond to poverty with visible actions cannot end it. The real solution to poverty also needs to be invisible. Every day on TV, we see people showing off how they must help poor children or poor people in Africa, India and so on, but despite trillions spent in alleviating poverty, the percentage of poor people is increasing in those parts of the world, and in the world in general.

On the other hand, where mind-transforming programs have taken place to change people from within, poverty has decreased. Where? You may ask. Singapore, South Korea, etc. Look around and see where people are more confident in themselves and their abilities.

Without a doubt, the invisible causes of poverty or success reside within each person. This, again, is why all programmes to alleviate poverty will continue to fail because structural programmes will never substitute peoples' minds, and their ability to think.

Poverty alleviation programmes should, therefore, focus on changing people's mindset. They should concentrate on transforming minds, motivating individuals to focus on their inner potential, and encourage them to use their heads rather than their hands. Hands alone have not solved their problems. Giving people the ability to think, and not just the capacity to eat, will help them to become free from hunger and make them better off. Those who think right will live right and will never go hungry.

The ability to have dominion, to subdue, to supply, to multiply and to replenish the earth is within everyone's reach. The outer manifestation of those things is just a sort of outlet, a warehouse of finite products. These products are neither made nor conceived there.

The external world - the world of the visible - is the end of the chain of creativity and productivity. You can only see and touch what has already been conceived and made. There are no limits to what can be conceived, but people's fear and discouragement limit what they can accomplish. The conception is the priority and privilege of the mind. Therefore, the mind should be protected and preserved.

The unconscious mind is virtually perfect and has no limits as to what can be drawn from it. The conscious mind is imperfect and suspect. The subconscious mind stores and retrieves data. Its job is to ensure that you respond correctly the way you are programmed to respond. Your

subconscious mind makes everything you say and do fit a pattern, consistent with your self-concept, your master program. If you program in the spirit of poverty, poverty will manifest outwardly. If you program in thoughts of health and happiness, it will release good health and happiness. As such, the subconscious mind is subjective. It does not think or reason independently; it merely obeys the commands it receives from your conscious mind. Just as your conscious mind can be thought of as the gardener who plants seeds, your subconscious mind can be thought of as the garden, or fertile soil, in which the seeds germinate and grow.

Your conscious mind commands and your subconscious mind obeys. **Your subconscious mind is an unquestioning servant that works day and night to make your behaviour fit a pattern consistent with your emotionalised thoughts, hopes, and desires. Your subconscious mind grows either flowers or weeds in the garden of your life. Whichever you plant, you create the mental equivalents.**

If you start considering your subconscious as a garden, you may as well start planting what

you want to reap. If you want wealth, plant in thoughts of wealth, and if you want to manifest abundance, plant in the seeds of abundance. Constantly think about and visualise what you want to see in your life. The more you do this, the more you will create in your subconscious the conditions for their manifestation.

Your subconscious mind causes you to feel emotionally and physically uncomfortable whenever you attempt to do anything new or different. In other words, when you want to change established patterns of behaviour, there is resistance. For example, when you want to learn a musical instrument, your mind resists because it is not used to it.

You can feel your subconscious pulling you back toward your comfort zone each time you try something new. Even thinking about doing something different will make you feel tense and uneasy.

High achievers are always stretching themselves, pushing themselves out of their comfort zones. They are very aware of how quickly the comfort zone, in any area, becomes a trap for them. The refusal to stretch is the reason why people are stuck in jobs they do not like and perform so poorly. People are stuck in poverty despite their daily disdain for poverty. **The ability to surpass the comfortable and self-imposed limitations is latent in everyone. By reprograming their subconscious, they can reprogram their lives. To get what you want from life, you need to make a conscious demand to your subconscious. Repeat your request until you have obtained what you want.**

The subconscious is a benevolent soldier who is always at work for us. It supplies and makes provisions for our benefit. But what it provides is nothing other than what we have planted. Abundance, ease, perfection, and progress are the effects of what one has created in the antechamber of his subconscious mind. What we see, as we already know, is not real or permanent. It depends entirely on the degree to which we cease to depend upon our consciousness or conscious mind dictating to us what it sees, hears, feels, touches or tastes.

Our psychic life is dependent upon the subconscious. So are our greatest gifts and achievements. The origin of our greatest realisations rests in our mind and our ability to press upon it for pure and perfect thoughts. The power of inspiration, forewarning, foresight, and discoveries are in our mind and most of what we can do lies within the subconscious.

Wrong thoughts, wrong suggestions, wrong focus, fear, worry, poverty, diseases, derive from wrong suggestions that are accepted by our subconscious mind. An alert and trained conscious mind can entirely prevent these wrong thoughts from entering the realm of the unconscious, by mounting guard and protection.

Conscious that man can train his mind to release the miraculous, Ben set up a mind transformation programme based on the following modules:

- Be yourself
- Dream big: reach for the stars
- Believe in your deity and potential
- Focus your efforts and change your mind-set
- Have faith in an idea and believe without any doubt that it is attainable
- Decide on your purpose
- Love the eternal, love yourself and love your neighbours

- Love your country and love your fellow citizens
- Prioritise greater causes
- Think like someone who is making the world a better place
- Train your mind, take inspiration and respect achievers
- Select a mentor, whether alive or dead, and aim to be like him
- Simulate regular meetings with your mentors
- See yourself where you want to be
- Write down your plans and goals and make up your mind to reach them
- Start pursuing your goals and plans immediately; don't procrastinate
- Be persistent and do not give up hope
- Be the change you want to see and reject poverty
- This is the plan for a university, solely dedicated to mind transformation.
- Constantly visualise what you need and what you want
- Constantly confess what you want to see happen and it will happen.
- Understanding the power of the subconscious
- Understanding your invisible power within
- Dream big or die small

Chapter 22

A personal pledge to seek the answers.

True wealth is within, and you have it, and to find the path, tune in for answers.

To improve, you need to change, and true change comes from within when you tune in.

To get what you want, you need to understand the right slant. So, tune in.

The power within is greater than the power without. The cause within reflects that without. So, to understand the real, tune in.

Your spiritual hands are more powerful than your physical hands. Your spiritual hands are the only tools you must grasp what you need in life. For guidance, tune in.

Visualise how you want your life to be. The way to do this is to tune in.

Your mind sees no boundaries. Nothing is beyond your reach, and everything is possible. So, tune in to achieve to seemingly impossible.

What you see within is true, but without faith it appears out of reach. Pursuing your dreams is a risk worth taking. If you lack inspiration, tune in.

Your zeal determines your faith. The right thoughts guide your faith; from within you, see the real; So, tune in.

You may not know how to apply your faith, but you are equipped to find the right answers. So, tune in.

How can you be confident that you can achieve your dreams? This causes fear. To know you can just look around. Others have done much more; so, can you. To get a glimpse, tune in.

You may be wondering how and when, but if you want, you can. For guidance, tune in.

Those who have achieved great things are ordinary people like you. You have the same faculties. So, to know your purpose, tune in.

No one was meant to fail. You have dominion over the earth, and your mission is to subdue,

POOR LAND OR POOR MINDS

multiply and replenish. If you fail, you are unfair to others. So, play your part. For directions, tune in.

Everything is ready and awaiting your call. Look around with your inner eyes; you are not far from the solution. Stay focussed and tune in for instructions.

Believe, plan and act. These steps are critical for you success. To understand what you need, tune in.

Today I believe I am here to fill a place, my place and without my deeds, the void will remain. If I am confused, I will tune in.

Today I take my pen to write down my life's goals. I will write all the good things that flow from within and remain tuned in for more. I'll stay in tune for the unending flow.

Though my goals may be large, I will proceed one step at a time. For inspiration, I will stay tune with the infinite.

My mind remains opened to reshape my goals. The right and noble goals are within. To discover more, I will tune in.

If I see the end from the start, there is no doubt; I will reach my goals. If in doubt, I will tune in.

The bigger the plan, the more I believe; if I dig within, I brave any obstacle so that I will remain in tune.

My purpose on earth was shaped before I was born; what I need to know is where I am going, and the answer is within. So, I stay in tune.

If I focus on starting right now without delay and with what I have, I will reach my goals. Most of what I need, I know not, but I will tune in for answers.

What I have now is good enough to start. So, I will start without delay, drawing on my inner strength. Without fail, I will stay tuned.

My life is mine, and I am the one to make it better. I have all the answers to the challenges I will face. To overcome them, I will stay tuned.

Because I have the tools I need to thrive, I will use them to the maximum. The secret is to stay tuned.

Today is a new day. I now know that I have God's attributes; to activate them, I will stay tuned to the source.

From today, all I need is within my reach. Nothing is impossible if I have faith. I am tuned in and remain in tune.

There are no limits to a divine supply, and all I need is within my reach. I am in tune with the divine.

I tune within for the wealth I possess. How great I am! I will not settle for less because I know my worth.

For all I want is prepared for me. I can get it if I want it with all my heart. I am longing for it, so, I will tune into the source.

I stretch my hands of faith to clutch what my sprit shows me. I do this well when I am in tune with the infinite.

I use words to convey what I want to achieve. This is the rule and reward for tuning in.

For all I will come to pass. For what I declare on earth is sealed above, when I am in tune with the Holy Spirit.

I am counted amount the elects and selected few because I am in tune with the infinite.

My wealth is part of a divine supply, for what I have will enrich the world, so I will tune in for more.

Everyone's success is good for all. Each can succeed if they are in tune with the divine.

I am positive and grateful. If all succeed, all will gain. Other people's success does not infringe my right to succeed. If I am lost, I will tune in for guidance.

Everyone can succeed if they are in tune with you, for in each person your spirit dwells. The secret is simple: tune in.

Because I am made in God's image, all that comes from me reflects God's goodness; all I need is be in tune.

Love in me commands to give to anyone, without a thought of being wronged. I will tune in for more to give and to forgive.

Love sees no faults. True love can be inspired when we are in tune with the source of love.

As I work towards my perfection, so do my brothers and sisters. So, I will remain in tune to perfect my ways.

I see in others the best and close my eyes to the wrong of now. For I learn from the king how to forgive and stay in tune to appease my hurts.

For tomorrow those who hurt me yesterday will become the best, provided they have tuned in for light.

Today is the day the world will know the benefits of my thoughts when I put into practice, what I have seen from within, when I am in tune.

All I need is within my reach, and my focus is within. I will stay in tune.

Your mind in me guides my steps, for what is wrong is not from you. To know your thoughts, I need to tune in.

Because I am like you, I see no wrong and speak no evil. My focus is to stay in tune.

I have here and now all I need to improve my life. My source withers not and is within and where I tune.

I am the best in all I do and get the best from all I see because I am in tune with the infinite.

I am more than able, and attract favours, as the good in me guides my steps, but I will remain in tune with the source of good.

As I stretch my faith and grow, the more I know the power within and the more I will stay tuned in.

So, through me the world will be a better place to live; this is the reason why I was born. To discover my real place, I will remain tuned.

I give more to those who pay for the gifts I have in me. I need to exercise this gift that is revealed when I am in tune with the divine.

I refuse to receive without giving back, because my nature is to give, and without pay back, I am useless to the world. The strategy is within, so I'll stay tuned.

I know there is more than my eyes can see; all this is within me. I will see the pure realities and the truths when I am in tune with the infinite.

I believe I am a gift to the world, so I want to do my bit, and the secret is to be in tune with the source.

I give thanks because today is a great day. Step by step I reach my goal.

The plan in my heart will come to pass. I will achieve my goals one by one before I leave the earth, provided I give up not. I will try and try and try until I succeed. So, I will stay in tune with the infinite for inspiration.

Enjoying today is part of the plan. Nothing can stop me from reaching my destination.

As I learn about my purpose, I tune within for a glimpse of light.

As I listen, the more I hear the voice guiding me from within.

I am grateful because I am alive. I am grateful, for I know I am a gift to the world. I will not miss the mark if I stay in tune.

If I am here, I will not stop giving my best, because, through me, other peoples' needs will be met.

Today is a new day to work smarter and enjoy life to the full. I am here to enjoy, not to endure. I will be a stranger to scarcity and poverty if I remain in tune.

With all the supplies I need at my reach, I will stretch my hands to grab all I need and want, and use my tongue to say what I see in my spirit, and all will come to pass, just as I declare and decree.

For sure, my decrees become a norm for what I want to see. Therefore, I will tune in.

My words are true, and what I say takes shape and becomes a reality. I declare aloud: "Today my life has changed for good, and from now, the world will hear from me, not because I want the fame, but because I want to share what I have to improve people's lives".

I take my place and work towards fulfilling my purpose. I will give and give if I have more to give. The more I give, the more I will receive. I will leave a legacy to the world and an inheritance to my children's children. I have come to know my source. When one taps into the divine supply, a legacy is left for future generations.

My possessions are part of the plan, for all to enjoy and not endure. No one was made to suffer or to be poor. There is a source of wealth within each person. Just tune in to find it!

Whether you are from a remote village like Fotetsa or Sekou, you have within you what it takes to be great. Poverty is not part of your nature. You were created for success, and the secret to that success is within you. So, TUNE IN.

End Notes

All the cities and villages cited in this book are real places. I preferred to use real rather than fictitious names as an attempt to raise awareness of the existence of some of the remotest places, which nonetheless represent areas of incomparable natural beauty. Africa is full of beautiful places and has the most beautiful names. Each name means something, and I am sure that some of you would want to know more about Fotetsa, Dschang, Santchou, Bale etc.

Please, feel free to search the location of each of these places on the Internet. I have been to some of the remotest places in the continent and this is my own way of bringing some of these places to life, and make readers discover them.

Dschang, Fotetsa, Santchou, Melong, for example, are in Cameroon, whereas, Zagtouli, Tenkodogo are the names of real places in Burkina Faso.

Blurb

Human nature rejects poverty, and everyone is made for success; controversially most human beings are poor. Nonetheless, everyone who grasps the secret of success will always be better off, and this secret is within everyone's reach. Your mind is the storehouse of success and failure.

People mistakenly think that the wealth of the land determines the wealth of citizens. This is not true because citizens create wealth that makes the nation rich. Likewise, poverty is also a condition created by people. To understand why people are rich or poor, we must understand how they think. This observation shows that poverty is created by a state of mind rather than the state of place.

Any place, anywhere in the world can change its fortune with a change of people's mind-set and the right application of knowledge.

The ability of an individual to think is a way by which he can enact and impose his will on earth, thus changing his social conditions. This book is for everyone who wants to get out of his shell and break the barriers of self-limitations. Therefore, for Africa to regain its place of predilection as a thinker, Africans must change the way they think.

Poverty is not in a place; poverty is in the minds.

About the author

Michel Ngue-Awane is a Commercial, change and transformation consultant (Procurement and Commissioning) and a political strategist. Michel is an innovative, dynamic and forward-thinking individual with a background in Philosophy, Psychology, Theology and Business. He a member of the Chartered Institute of Purchasing and Supply (CIPS) and holds a Bachelor and master's in philosophy and Politics, and he obtained his MBA from London Metropolitan University before starting a professional Doctorate in Social Work at Tavistock & Portman NHS, which he deferred to focus on his business. He also holds a Diploma in Christian Ministries from KCE.

As an author and political strategist with extensive knowledge on African Politics, he is regularly invited on various TV and radio networks, both in Europe and in Africa as a consultant on African issues and politics.

He has published other books such as:

- Practice Guide to Social Housing 2009, acclaimed by housing professionals in the United Kingdom.
- Above the Colonial Subconscious, Africa Moves 2015

Upcoming books

- The Wind of Change
- The Way Forward
- African Explorers through the Mediterranean and the Red Sea
- And, if God hated Africa (Et Si Dieu detestait L'Afrique!)
- Africa, The Way and The Pain- L'Afrique, Le Chemin et la Douleur.

Michel runs some different businesses including his brand PEP Chilli Sauce, which is sold across the UK and Europe, and he has written over 100 songs.

Ge is also the COE of Cameroon Britain Business Council, The African Britain Business Council and Director of M.N. AWANE Consulting Ltd, MichelN. Awane Ltd.